Are you a creative NUT?

Celebrating Difference, Understanding Genius & How to Operate in this world

STEVE FAVELL

Copyright © 2024 Steve Favell. All rights reserved. No portion of this book may be reproduced mechanically, electronically, or by any other means, including photocopying, without written permission of the author/publisher. It is illegal to copy this book, post it to a website, either in part or wholly, or distribute it by any other means without prior permission from the author/publisher in writing.

The moral right of the author has been asserted.

ISBN: 9798323801213

Steve Favell

Felixstowe, Suffolk United Kingdom

Book cover design by Alishba Shah

Published by In View Publishing

Limits of Liability and Disclaimer of Warranty

The author and publisher shall not be liable for your misuse of this material. This book is strictly for informational and entertainment purposes. The author and/or publisher shall have neither liability nor responsibility to anyone with respect to any loss or damage caused, or alleged to be caused, directly or indirectly by the information contained in this book.

DEDICATION

I'd like to dedicate this book to Mary Favell, my late mother who always believed in me, encouraged me and made my world a happy one by praising each small achievement.

Steve Favell

STEVE FAVELL

ACKNOWLEDGMENTS

"There was a time in my past when I sat at a table with a bottle of whisky, a packet of Diazepam and a handful of Prozac. In my case sadly it cost me my daughter who, to this day, won't speak to me because I let her down so badly. I was so self-absorbed I wasn't there for her when she needed me. Something I have to live with, and I cannot express the pain I hold inside or the love for her which I cannot share."

I'd like to thank both my wonderful wife Stephanie and In View Publishing for your guidance and patience. This book would never have seen the light of day without the encouragement you gave me.

Steve Favell

CONTENTS

DEDICATION III

ACKNOWLEDGMENTS V

FORWARD I

INTRODUCTION VII

CHAPTER 1 1

UNDERSTANDING YOUR GENIUS 1

CHAPTER 2 7

FINDING OUT WHO YOU REALLY ARE 7

CHAPTER 3 21

LETTING PEOPLE INTO YOUR WORLD............................. 21

CHAPTER 4 47

THE POWER OF A WORD 47

CHAPTER 5 51

THE MISUNDERSTOOD PERSONALITY............................. 51

CHAPTER 6 59

WHY WE CAN'T THINK IN NEGATIVES 59

CHAPTER 7 65

LET'S TALK ABOUT SEX 65

CHAPTER 8 75

UNDERSTANDING YOUR TIME MANAGEMENT 75

CHAPTER 9 81

TAKING OWNERSHIP.. 81

CHAPTER 10 85

GETTING OUT FROM UNDER THE CIRCUMSTANCES 85

CHAPTER 11... 93

MAKING YOUR PLAN OF ACTION.. 93

CHAPTER 12 97

DESIGNING YOUR FUTURE 97

CHAPTER 13 105

HANDLING AND UNDERSTANDING FEAR 105

CHAPTER 14 111

MAKING YOUR PERFECT EXISTENCE 111

CHAPTER 15 117

CREATING ANOTHER LIFETIME 117

THAT STARTS TODAY.. 117

CHAPTER 16 123

HOW TO DEVELOP REAL WISDOM...123

AFTERWORD 139

ABOUT THE AUTHOR 142

FORWARD

In the early 60's, Steve was living in the small village of Clifton in Bedfordshire. Life was basic and education was still quite draconian. To set the scene, ball point pens were not in common use, so children still used ink pens filled from a pot of ink. Computers, mobile phones and digital anything didn't exist and along with being a bit 'special', as Steve was so often described, being left-handed also wasn't recognised by his teachers. For that matter, nor were many of the conditions which we see as commonplace today such as dyslexia. He was forced by his teachers to write instead with his right hand. Regularly his sister was called at the end of the school day to witness Steve getting the cane across his hands for "His appalling writing and his unwillingness to read properly!" With each swipe would come the phrase "You must try harder!"

Being branded special and even called lazy and stupid by the education system continued when he moved to his middle school in Hitchen in Hertfordshire. It was there that Steve first encountered the Dunce's class. A class especially for those who were branded stupid and disruptive. It was a room where little or no teaching went on and the focus was on discipline. Keeping the class quiet to allow the 'good' children to concentrate in their classrooms.

Steve never intended to be a naughty boy. His disruptiveness was simply that he questioned everything. His logical mind needed to understand before he would accept and process the information. He also had the tendency to tap rhythmically on his desk as though it were a drum. Often Steve would do this at school with rulers because it made him feel calm and he found he could also count by doing this. Whilst this is something he now tends to hide; this drumming is something he still does. It was no surprise therefore, that in later life, he became a percussionist.

As a result of his 'persistent behaviour', even more common slurs were aimed at Steve throughout his schooling. "Have you got verbal diarrhoea?!" as he was always talking and asking questions. He was also called a "Sod! Banging on the desk to annoy everyone!" The latter often also got him the cane or slipper (a rubber plimsoll) across his backside in front of the class, sometimes with his trousers pulled down.

Today we wouldn't condone this attitude and it would be seen as physical and mental abuse of a minor. As you might imagine it didn't take long before Steve started to believe he was, indeed, stupid.

For the most part his past remains bottled up inside him, although the abuse he received during his schooling still affects him to this day. Perhaps, because of that abuse, Steve has grown into a people pleaser. In his younger years he suffered for a long time with social anxiety, a fear of what people might think of him or how they would judge him.

You might ask why his parents didn't intervene. He was, after all, one of five children who were loved, supported and encouraged by his family. The answer is simple - they didn't know. Like so many other children who are abused or are witnesses to the abuse, Steve and his sister didn't tell their parents. His sister also still carries the scars and the feelings of guilt from their schooldays together. But they were children, and these were adults, so in their minds who would dare to question teachers?

For all of his challenges, like others who are deemed 'different' from the majority, who are seen as 'special', even at that young age Steve also had many exceptional talents. During his early days at senior school, he would sneak into the main school hall at lunchtime to secretly practice playing on their shiny grand piano. Unfortunately, one day he was caught by a teacher. As a result, the very next day and in front of the whole school at assembly the headmaster announced to everyone, "It seems during lunch breaks Master Stephen Favell has been messing about on our most valuable Blüthner piano!"

Calling Steve to the front of the assembled crowd of school children the headmaster continued, "If you will be so good as to come up the front Favell and show us what you can do, we would appreciate it." Eleven-year-old Steve was mortified and sat with his head bowed. Undeterred the Headmaster shouted, louder this time, "Come on boy, up you come!"

In those days it wasn't cool to play the piano. In fact, you were considered to be a sissy if you did. Slowly Steve stood up and made his way to the grand piano enduring the taunts from the head in a sarcastic tone, "Hurry boy we are all waiting to hear the maestro!"

Sitting down on the huge piano stool, (Steve was only just over 4ft tall at that age) he proceeded to flawlessly perform two movements from Bach's *Anna Mary Magdalene Notebook*, stunning the assembled audience into silence. A silence only broken eventually by the headmaster pronouncing, "Ha! That shocked you all didn't it? Thought it would." This experience gave Steve his first taste of self-pride and the hunger to undertake public performances. It also gave him a lesson in how sometimes people twist the truth and take credit to save face.

As he grew up Steve has overcome his difficulties in communication, and his challenges with his own self-worth. He has become an accomplished musician performing at thousands of venues whilst, at the same time, developing one of the country's most successful musical instrument retail companies.

In his early 40's he left the music retail world to turn his attention to the world of National sales. He built and trained two highly successful National sales organisations and went on to do the same with several training companies. Eventually Steve worked as a Business Manager for an FE College. He increased its income by over £1.5 million in the very first year.

With a passion for psychology and a personal understanding of the value of being different, a NUT as he describes himself, Steve has become a highly respected coach helping countless numbers of people overcome their challenges to achieve their goals in both their businesses and in their personal lives.

Stephanie Mackentyre

Podcaster, Presenter & Writer

STEVE FAVELL

INTRODUCTION

A NUT

N - Nonpareil - Having no equal or rival for excellence or desirability.

U – Unrecognised Unicity – Uniqueness being misunderstood or not seen.

T – Thole - To endure; to suffer.

When I was a young boy, on a regular basis I had tantrums which as a family we now laugh about. I used to run upstairs slam the door, lock myself in the bathroom, and then lifting the toilet seat I would shout every obscenity and horrid thing I could think of down the toilet and flush it away. This was in the hopes that my mum wouldn't hear. Of course she did, as did everyone else, so she would spank me.

The point here is that as a creative, someone with an inventive, arty type of mind, I share, along with most creatives the challenge that most of my life I have been described as, 'Highly Strung.' Affected by mood swings, experiencing incredible highs and very low, lows. As a good friend once put it to me, I was as 'nutty as a fruitcake!' It took me years to become mellow and to bring myself into balance. So, if you are also as 'nutty as a fruit cake' then, welcome to my world. The first step on your journey is to understand you are not alone and as a creative, it's normal.

Us NUTS do, however, have to live in this world, so I hope this book will help you to navigate your day to day. If, as you read on, you find you are not a NUT then I hope this will help you to understand better, those of us who are.

We are all different, as a NUT or if you have a NUT in your life, you will identify with certain aspects of this book, but other traits won't relate to you at all. The point is, those aspects that are not you, do describe others who you will be interacting with. As you read on, see if you can identify those traits in other people that you know.

It is a sad fact that many of us are subjected to abuse from others and sometimes it's inflicted just because we are seen as different. If you have in the past, or you are now, suffering abuse I am truly sorry. My heart goes out to you, and I pray that you find the strength to get the help and support you so badly need. Abuse is not acceptable, and you should not tolerate it. You are worth so much more than that. I hope this book will help you understand who you are and how you can change your situation.

In my case, yes, I was spanked by my mother but in those days, it was normal for children to be spanked. Please don't fall into the trap of believing that I was somehow damaged by that or that my mother was an abuser. She never actually hurt me mentally or physically. What she did was to give me structure and boundaries which I needed. Otherwise, as a highly strung child, I would most probably have been completely wayward.

Looking after my father, five children and her aged mother, life for my mother was tough and, in those days, it was perfectly normal to spank a child to keep them in line. Her token spank was not abuse, it was symbolic. Some of the thrashings we got at school however were abuse and could be quite painful and yes, I do see and agree, there is a difference. Particularly the mental abuse I received at school, did leave a mark on me. In many ways that's why I've written this book to share how I came to terms with it and how you can to. We should not tolerate physical or mental abuse, that's why, as a society, we need to take stock of what we are subjecting others and ourselves to on a daily basis.

Our brains are programmed by what we see, what we touch, what we smell, what we hear, what we read and our experiences. In my early years I was a boy scout and as such, like most of my friends, I carried a knife. In the '60s we were encouraged to. We got badges for our woodcraft, and we learnt how to cut and make knots out of ropes.

I was also a paper boy, up early every morning rain or shine to push newspapers through doors to earn a few bob. That enabled me to thumb through the Exchange and Mart advertising newspaper drooling over the expensive Swiss army knives which had bottle openers and screwdrivers as well as multiple blades in their handles. However, the idea of stabbing someone never crossed our minds. It would have been abhorrent to us.

When I was at middle school, at Halesworth in Suffolk, my family home was next to the Rifle Hall. The Rifle Hall was an old dance hall with a bar and a large stage where most Saturdays I'd go with my friends to see a live band. In the '60s and '70s most young people couldn't afford a car so even small towns like Halesworth had a dance hall with discos or regular bands travelling to perform at them.

As boys we'd all strut about eyeing up the girls whilst they would dance round their handbags, clutching their rum and blacks which their boyfriends had bought for them in the hope of a snog. Well, that's the mental image I call to mind, at least.

On one such occasion, to show off to the girls, my friend and I play-acted a fight scene on the steps outside the hall. He was the angry threatening macho man; I was to be the passive hero. On this occasion for effect, he pulled his knife threatening me. He had no intention of using it, he knew it, so did I. Unfortunately, I had been watching Bruce Lee Kung Foo films on the television. So, for maximum effect, I attempted to kick the knife from his hand. The shock on his face when his knife stuck in my leg! That did hurt and my babyish whining and tears put the girls off me for the rest of the term! I still have the scar on my leg to prove it.

In today's Britain, we have banned spanking to stop those would-be abusers. We have banned smoking in public places to stop harm to others. We have introduced laws, even on speech, so why then are we constantly abusing our children and ourselves by subjecting our brains, programming them to see violence and gore as normal by allowing very realistic graphic video games that promote violence? I believe this is one of the main reasons that, even very young children, often now seem to have no fear of stabbing someone or violently hurting others. After all they do it all the time online and it looks real. Where am I going with this?

It's a reminder to us creatives, us NUTS, us geniuses – yes, we can create the most fantastic powerful things but, in doing so we also have a responsibility to consider the effects and how they should be policed. It's also a reminder to us not to fill our brains with harmful content because we can be the worst offenders for drowning our brains in rubbish as a distraction from life. This can be harmful to our state of mind, effectively abusing our own minds.

In this book you will find a lot about psychology, helping you to understand who you are and how we can change our situation but, for the psychology to do so, you will need to implement and practice these changes.

Here's an example:

A friend of mine was on the golf course playing a round of golf. Unbeknownst to him a very famous pro golfer was watching him and eventually approached my friend. "I hope you don't mind." He said, "I've been watching you; you have real talent but the way you are standing and holding the club is wrong. If you let me show you how to stand better, I can guarantee it will improve your game."

My friend of course let the pro golfer show him how to stand and hold the club and then having thanked him, started to play that way. The challenge was a new way of standing and holding the club which my friend found was uncomfortable at first. It wasn't what he was used to, but he had the good sense to persevere and keep practicing that way until it became comfortable. The outcome, my friend is now a pro golf teacher.

CHAPTER 1

UNDERSTANDING YOUR GENIUS

In this world everyone is different. Oh yes, we have similar looks and personality types. There are loads of books on this but, the truth is our biggest differences are the various hang-ups we each have and how we deal with them.

Often this manifests itself in the way we deal and react to others and situations but, in my experience, I have found the saying 'Genius borders on insanity' can be so true.

Many of the best and certainly all the most gifted musicians I have worked with seem to have personality challenges and often bouts of depression. The vast majority of inventive successful business people seem to be "odd characters" often lacking empathy or subject to bursts of anger and frustration. Artists are often referred to as "Out There" "Hippies" or "Odd balls" and Maths/IT geniuses seen as "Geeks."

But here is the thing: Us NUTs are the main movers and shakers in this world. We are the ones that make things happen, we are the innovators not just imitators. The problem solvers. We create new concepts, build empires and are the joy givers, making music, films and art.

One of the best guitar players I ever worked with, let's call him Rob, used to have episodes where before a performance, he would just wander off. Looking back now I can see he was probably so stressed about walking out on stage that it was his way of calming down and preparing himself for the performance. At the time it was very annoying as the rest of us in the band had to unload the vans, set up all the sound gear and lights and then do a sound check without him. On stage he was magnificent, brilliant, a genius. He could be your best pal with a heart of gold but, at other times, he could be your worst nightmare.

We were doing a performance at a venue near the sea front which had a particularly difficult, what in the performance world we call a 'get in', i.e. it was really difficult to access and carry our musical equipment to the stage and to get set up. This particular venue, which better remain nameless, was well known for the number of steep steps up to the stage entrance and the stage manager was a real jobsworth. He was paranoid about doors being left open so, we had to open and close the doors every time which is not easy when you are carrying very large, heavy speakers, especially up concrete stairs.

We had just finished a long run of shows and were all exhausted. We arrived, parked the vans and Rob wandered off.

To say we were cheesed off with him would be a huge understatement. It was a ridiculously hot day, and we had no choice but to set up without him. Exhausted we did the sound check and waited for him, getting more and more annoyed. After a while it got too much for us, so we decided to go and find him and have it out with him. Experience told us he would probably wander through the sand dunes and, as it was such a hot day, he'd probably go for a swim. Sure enough, just as we got deep into the sand dunes, we came across his clothes. Rob truly was a genius he wrote all the arrangements for the band, designed the stage set, choreographed the performances and could improvise to fit with any musician in any style of music. He also had the most remarkable memory. Rob truly was a very rare talent, part of what is known as the 2% club.

However, finding his clothes we realised they included his pants, he had gone skinny dipping. So, we simply gathered his clothes up and took them back with us to the dressing room and then waited. We laughed; he would have no alternative but to cross the road naked in front of the queuing audience. We knew he would never miss a performance and would do whatever it took to be on stage even if he was a pain in the ass, so we weren't worried he'd not turn up.

Upon reflection, although we didn't see it at the time, the rest of us were all NUTs. We all had our issues, and we could all be difficult, its true to say we were being just as intolerant as people often were to us. At the time we didn't consider his challenges and coping mechanism. That is something I often now reflect on when others are intolerant with me.

Sitting in the dressing room we waited and waited and then 20 minutes before we were due to go on stage the door flung open and in walked Rob, fully clothed. Unfortunately, we had stolen someone else's clothes!

There are lots of statistically rare people in this world. Just 10% are left-handed. 11% percent have naturally curly hair and only 4% have naturally blond hair. But as a NUT you are especially rare. With over seven billion people on this planet only 2% are those that make things happen. 60% watch things happen and the rest wonder what the hell did happen!

This last group will go through their lives falling into a job, with a 'glass half empty' attitude, never striving to achieve anything, just settling for whatever comes their way. I call them the 'settle fors.'

As part of the 2% club, that make things happen, about 140 million of us to be more precise, you are statistically just one in every 50. There is however another 2% group on the planet. Those who have green eyes. If you also have green eyes then congratulations, you are one of the rarest people on the planet.

The middle group, the 60%, are those that do want more, will work hard but most will never quite get into the 2% because they are the fence walkers. Sitting in their comfort zones watching you as you strive to achieve stuff and push the boundaries. A few will join you because you inspire them to do so but, at times the 60% group can be your worst nightmares. Not because they intentionally want to be, it's just, as you take chances and strive to push the boundaries, as you try new things, they are reminded that they are not doing it themselves. You are like a thorn in their side. You make them feel uncomfortable about themselves. They have a tendency to put you down saying things like, "You'll never do that" or "Don't be disappointed if it doesn't work out." It's their justification for their own inaction.

For the same reasons, there are also the ones that, when you do achieve results, will say, "Wow, you were lucky!" or "You got in just at the right time" or even, "I wish I had your luck!" Truth is, you simply remind them that they are not doing it themselves.

Here's the good and bad news. As a creative NUT you have the ability to do great things, to build yourself and others a fantastic life. To make a real difference in this world and become so much more than the average person. However, in doing this you have to deal with you!

6

CHAPTER 2

FINDING OUT WHO YOU REALLY ARE

Now I must say, it took years before I could honestly say that I really know who I am, what I am like and the challenges I have. Nowadays, people seem to see me as a calm, lovely, caring person who is so helpful and wonderful. They really do. Yes, I've learnt to be a great conman, able to hide my challenges. Able to get others to see the good side of me and not see all the crap in my head I deal with every day and the bad thoughts I can still have. Over time I've learnt how to calm myself, to sleep away challenging periods and to use my genius for the good of others, which has given me a purpose in life. To be honest, I can also now manipulate people and situations to get my way. I am able to get others to think they did it themselves. Rather than how I used to be, constantly butting heads with people.

I must say it's a great feeling when you have mastered it!

As a NUT you may also suffer from a fundamental challenge that most of us have. We understand that to be understood, we need to associate with other creatives also to learn and feed our creativity, we need to associate with others very much like us. The old adage rings true here, "If you want to be an alcoholic, go to a pub and hang about with alcoholics." "If you want to be a drug addict, find some drug addicts and hang about with them." Works every time! So, if you want to be a great artist, writer, musician, inventor, or business leader you need to hang about with those that are in life where you want to be, those that you admire and look up to.

But ….

When we hang about with other creatives, we often forget that other NUTs are like us, they are subject to mood swings and have their own unique challenges too. Knowing this, why is it we can so easily let ourselves get upset and hurt when they don't react or respond the way we want them to? Why do we get bent out of shape when we ask others for their opinions or we show them our work and they give their honest, subjective, but constructive criticism?

In the same way that we can get upset, we can also so easily upset other people when they ask us to give them constructive feedback. Chances are we probably don't realise how much other people can look up to us and really value our opinion. With the intention of being helpful, we can have the tendency to bluntly do just as they have asked of us. We say it as it is and then they throw a wobbly because they didn't like what we had to say.

This is often the case with family members, our parents, our children, our loved ones. It can be our mentors and those we most look up to. It can be just about anyone. The thing is, we are all different and, in some ways, we are all NUTs. Everyone likes praise and to think what they have done is brilliant. No one likes to feel they are being put down, especially us NUTs.

You may remember, there was a very popular TV comedy sit com called Hi-de-Hi about the entertainment team, the Yellow Coats, at a holiday camp which they called Maplin's. Along with Ted Bovis the comedian and Jeffery Fairbrother the Entertainment Manager one of the main characters was a children's entertainer called Mr Partridge, brilliantly played by Leslie Dwyer. Mr Partridge hated children. The writers Jimmy Perry and David Croft also wrote Dad's Army (including the theme tune), It Ain't Half Hot Mum and You Rang M'Lord? They seemed to base characters on real people but as caricatures of them.

I often wondered if they based the character Mr Partridge on the real-life entertainment manager who, during the '60s and '70s, was at one of Gt Yarmouth's biggest holiday camps in Norfolk. Just like the character from Hi di Hi he too would say he hated children. In the '60s and '70s this particular Holiday camp was on the circuit for most up and coming artists like Shane Richie and Joe Pasquale. Holiday camps were one of the main stages for artists in the UK at that time. It was at the Butlin's Pwllheli holiday camp in Wales that Paul McCartney played to a live audience for the first time and Ringo Starr was with Rory Storm and the Hurricanes at a Butlin's holiday camp when he got the call to join the Beatles.

One of the acts that regularly performed with us at this holiday camp was the Webb Twins who also played the characters of Stanley and Bruce Matthews in Hi-de-Hi.

This particular entertainment manager had a very dry sense of humour and if you didn't know him, he could easily offend you. I remember the very first time I did a show for him, during the last number, during our big finale he walked on stage and unplugged the band, yes literally pulled the power plug out! Then over the house microphone he said, "That's enough of that it's time for the bingo." You can imagine, we were furious. As we left the stage, he turned to us and over the microphone he said, "You were rubbish, get off!" We were gutted. Even today as I write this, I can still feel those emotions from that night, the raw hurt.

When we got into the dressing room, almost in tears, the other acts were laughing. "We should have warned you." They said, "He does it to everyone, it's his thing, his sense of humour the audience love it!"

They were right, when you got to know him, he was the nicest man ever and brilliant at his job. It was his humour, part of his act but, you can imagine, a lot of people didn't take it well and he came in for a lot of stick from some of the other artists.

If you are like me, you may need and crave praise. Many of us have an elevated opinion of our abilities; we don't take criticism well and find it very hard to ever admit that we are wrong. Even something said in jest, even if we know it was said as a joke, can hurt us and stay with us for years.

To navigate this world, I have found that a good tactic is before opening my mouth, I first ask myself, does the person asking for an opinion really want one? Or are they actually seeking my approval and support? Then and only then, if I'm sure they do want my genuine opinion, and I feel the need to say something they might not like, I use a 'praise sandwich.' What I mean by a 'praise sandwich' is to always give the person praise before giving your opinion. Then give your opinion in the most positive encouraging way possible and then again give the person and their work some more praise. Therefore, the last thing you say is positive not negative… it seems to work.

So, the conversation might go like this …

"I love the overall mood that the piece sets and the way it flows, and your guitar part is exceptional but personally think the mid eight could do with a little more work. That said, it shows you are a real talent and I think it could be a huge hit."

Let us see if this is you

Have a look at the list and see how many apply: -

1. I often think, why should I bother?
2. I worry a lot.
3. I can be very clever.

4. People seem to look to me for solutions, often to things I think are quite simple.

5. Those people who look to me are often not there for me when I need them.

6. If I'm doing it, it needs to be perfect.

7. I struggle to understand my own feelings.

8. I don't trust others as much as I should because I might get hurt.

9. I avoid doing stuff that bores me.

10. I avoid doing stuff I worry about.

11. I am always worried about what others will think about me or how others will judge me. I also worry about how they will judge my work.

12. People see me as confident, often over-confident but they don't see how needy I really am.

13. I'm afraid I will push people away if I open up to them.

Results:

Answer Yes to 5 questions? Congratulations, you're a NUT.

7 to 9 Yes answers and you're a NUT's NUT

10 to 13 Yes answers, wow you're a super NUT!

Remember, all of us NUTs are geniuses so let's celebrate it!!

Here is the clever thing. Those of you that didn't get 5 yes answers are almost certainly in denial because the fact that you are still reading this, tells me you are also a NUT. You are part of the 2%, hungry for information, prepared to challenge yourself. You are just a different kind of NUT that's all.

In my head, I think that those who are not NUTs will have put this book down long ago. Those people didn't relate to any of it and instead have gone back to watching their favourite soaps on TV or reading some crappy rubbish about the 2% who, unlike them, are doing something with their lives. The 'settle fors'. They will probably also say this book is complete rubbish!

What Steve!!!! This isn't like you! You never say stuff like that …. Please don't be offended, the point I'm making here is, yes actually I do think like this sometimes. Many of us have problematic thoughts from time to time. We don't mean harm by it, its stuff that pops into our heads. It can be hurtful to others but is also often aimed at ourselves and our own most recent work. We'll look at it and say to ourselves, "Anyway this is all rubbish!"

One thing I've learnt is that if we say negative stuff out loud, the thoughts that just pop into our minds, then it will upset people and we will end up getting hurt. Although at times we can say what we think without using any emotional input or thinking it through, most of us find it hard to take criticism when it comes back in our direction.

Not every NUT is like this but for those of us who are, it goes like this: We say what we think, or actually, in most cases, we say what in that moment we can see logically to be true, and it upsets people. Their natural defence system kicks in and so they react negatively to us. In doing so, we soon learn we can easily push people away by being so outspoken.

The daft thing is, at times, when we feel cornered or are feeling down, we can even go into self-destruct mode. Saying the very things, we know will push people away and we can do it in the moment, on purpose. We then have to live with the consequences and, as we can be so stubborn, it's not unusual for us to never admit that we were wrong. Even though we know we are and even when the outcome is hurting us more than anyone else. That leads to my next list: -

1. It's me I am the problem.
2. I hate who I am, a lot of the time.
3. I'm useless.

Isn't it interesting that the song Anti-Hero by Taylor Swift was such a huge hit and resonated with so very many people? The song is full of low esteem and self-loathing,

I should not be left to my own devices
They come with prices and vices

I end up in crisis (tale as old as time)
I wake up screaming from dreaming
One day I'll watch as you're leaving
'Cause you got tired of my scheming

The empathy by so many for these words demonstrates these thoughts and feelings are common to most everyone at some point in their lives. It proves that when we have self-doubt and issues with self-worth, we are not alone. The words describe so many people's concerns about being or feeling they are different. The first line of the chorus especially sums up so many people's perception about themselves and their situation.

It's me, Hi, I'm the problem, it's me
At teatime, everybody agrees
I'll stare directly at the sun but never in the mirror
It must be exhausting always rooting for the anti-hero

The key message from this is that we all, at times in our lives, have self-doubt and question our self-worth. We tend to measure ourselves against others who we perceive to be better than us. But the truth is, they have or will have at some point had, just the same issues of low self-worth that we have. We are all different and we should celebrate that, celebrate who we are. We should embrace the value we each bring to the world and understand that in most cases the largest issue we actually have is that we don't feel valued, needed or that we don't have a purpose.

Most of us need to feel needed, need to feel that we are of value and have a purpose, a mission. A reason to exist. Something to work towards that means something to us as an individual. We can, if we are not careful, try to fill this void by following the advice of others. Doing what they see as their mission but, it's not ours, so it rarely works. There is also a danger that, to fill this void, we hook up with and support others who themselves are very needy. This happens a lot with relationships, having partners who need all our support and attention, but they do not encourage or support us in return and instead drag us down.

Most of us NUTs not only need to be needed but also need a lot of praise and encouragement. Ideally from someone with a strong character, who we can look up to, who can be our rock. Someone who takes a genuine interest in what we believe in, what our mission is and our Why! (I'll explain the Why! in a moment) Without this praise and support, drive and ambition will start to die, and depression often sets in.

Here's an example of what I mean …

It was a blistering hot day in ancient Rome, a lady was walking past a man sitting on the roadside bashing away at a stone. "What are you doing" she asked? The man looked up at her, his blistered face angry and unhappy. "I've got to cut these lumps of marble into squares, millions of them, it's going to take me the rest of my life and I'm paid a pittance, I hate my life." The lady walked on, turning the corner she came across another man doing exactly the same thing as the first. His face was blistered and burnt but he was singing, happy and smiling.

"What are you doing?" she asked, "I'm building a cathedral!" he replied.

Simon Sinek an English-born American author and inspirational speaker on business leadership famously talks about the "Why" the need for us to have a cause, a purpose a mission. Something we believe in, that we value. In some, this might be a religious cause but it's not about religion. As Simon puts it, *"If someone has a purpose, a cause, a vision they will happily work with blood and sweat and tears towards that goal but, if all they are doing is working for a paycheck then they won't feel valued or fulfilled."*

It may be that at some point you had a great boss who encouraged you, praised you, valued you and your work and made you feel what you were doing was worthwhile and of value. I bet you enjoyed the job and worked hard at it? If you have had the opposite, someone who didn't make you feel that what you were doing was of value and you saw no value in what you were doing, then I bet you hated the job and you also lacked motivation.

A twist on the Cinderella story is the brilliant film *Pretty Woman* with Julia Roberts and Richard Geer. It depicts a sex worker picked up by a rich, ruthless businessman who has made a fortune asset stripping businesses. As their relationship develops, he starts to see the value in her and slowly starts to treat her with the respect and encouragement that she deserves. At one point in the film, he sends her shopping with his debit card for some new, very expensive clothes and she goes into a smart boutique shop. Because of the way she looks they judge her to be of no value to them. They treat her with disrespect and refuse to serve her. How powerful it is then when she is able to return, dressed in the finest clothes, loaded down with shopping bags from other expensive boutiques. She goes into their shop and reminds them of their error saying, "Big mistake." As a NUT you might recognise this feeling of people judging you. How nice it is to be able to say to them "Big mistake" when you have proved them wrong. As someone once put it, *'Success is revenge.'*

In the film, Richard Geer falls in love with the woman she really is. She challenges him to be better, as he does her. She questions his values of truth and honesty and in return he gives her the gift of being valued. As the film progresses her self-worth and confidence grow, and she helps him see his true value, not only in himself, but also in his business. At first it is her that we see the need to change and grow but the very clever twist to the film is that she ends up changing him by helping him understand the value of having a real purpose in life that is of value to others. They stretch each other to grow to be better than they were and in doing so find real happiness.

To reach our potential we all need to be stretched as a person, to do something that challenges and excites us and that we believe in. If not our "can't be bothered" part of our brains becomes an issue. Us NUTs are usually a kind of adrenaline junkie, getting our fix from the stuff we do well, our creativity. Without it we can go into withdrawal and our withdrawal symptoms often include a lack of energy, lethargy and self-loathing.

There was a time in my past when I sat at a table with a bottle of whisky, a packet of Diazepam and a handful of Prozac. Thankfully for me, I was able to think, hang on what am I doing? I need to take back control of my life. The point I'm making here by being so upfront and honest with you is, we can let ourselves get so incredibly low that we go into self-destruct mode. In my case, sadly it cost me my daughter who, to this day, won't speak to me because I let her down so badly. I was so self-absorbed I wasn't there for her when she needed me. Something I have to live with, and I cannot express the pain I hold inside or the love for her which I cannot share.

Us NUTs do many things that we regret, it's part of who we are because we push boundaries and step outside convention. We have to learn to deal with the consequences and to live with our past as we strive to move forward. Yes, it can be very hard but it's part of the process and we must not let it define us or destroy us. Because destroy us it will, if we let it.

I like the saying,

'There is never a wrong time to do the right thing.'

One of the major challenges we and everyone else faces today is that it is now seen as totally undesirable, even unacceptable, to make mistakes and get things wrong. At school we are judged on how much we get right. At work we mustn't make mistakes. We mustn't say what we think in case it offends others and in doing all this we lose the opportunity to learn, develop and grow.

If someone holds a radical opinion, silencing them doesn't change their opinion; in fact, it might fuel it. Look at history and how persecuting people for their religious beliefs only drove those who were being persecuted to strengthen their resolve and, in many cases, this led to wars.

Society seems to have forgotten that advances are only made by listening to others who have different views and influencing others with love, compassion, understanding and education. As creatives it's in our nature to challenge the status quo, to push boundaries and seek proof rather than just to accept what we are told. We learn from the mistakes we make. It is those errors that enabled us to develop and advance and it is being prepared to listen to others, to gain an understanding of what other people think, that allows us to make advances in this world.

As creatives, we need to allow ourselves to make mistakes, to share our thoughts and conclusions with each other and the wider society so we can learn and, in turn, educate others.

CHAPTER 3
LETTING PEOPLE INTO YOUR WORLD

There was a time, in my case up until recently, where you wouldn't have been able to read this because having written it, I would have thrown it in the bin so no one could see it or judge it. Or judge me too I suppose. Like so many people, I've been afraid of exposing my true self or my work to others, even those closest to me.

Maslow's Hierarchy of Needs talks about how we each are at different stages of our lives and how we move between those stages. I'm not sure exactly where I am at the moment, but I have come to a stage where I no longer care about who sees what. No, that's actually not true, I do care but I *choose* not to care.

As a NUT we are easily bored of stuff, even our own stuff we create. If we create something good, then privately we like to look at it and marvel at our genius but then we quickly move on.

Often NUTs build brilliant businesses but then having had the excitement and challenge of building them we have to run them and that's boring, so we get depressed. The challenge here is that we are not good at delegation. We also get very frustrated trying to teach others stuff that's obvious to us. They just don't get it do they?

Let's face it, secretly we can at times see ourselves as being better or cleverer than most others. We are, after all, NUTs. The challenge therefore is we don't want to do an average job or be told what to do. Being told what to do, can after all be a trigger for us to have an 'episode'. An episode to me could be a panic attack, a confidence implosion or an outburst. It might have any number of physical symptoms like, pains, sickness or contraction of muscles and that's without the stress that it adds to.

When having one of these episodes, we might walk away from a task or purposely give a stupid argument to antagonise others, it's all part of our self-destruct mode. The silly thing about it is we do it because we are, as I've said earlier in this book, adrenaline junkies, looking for the next fix of excitement away from the boring. We need a purpose, a mission in life.

We also do it because we can feel we deserve it, because of what we have or haven't done in the past or because of how rubbish we think in that moment we are at something. Fight or flight mode creates adrenaline, so does pain and hurt.

Let me explain …

For years I have internally punished myself for failing my daughter, I still do. Pain can become in itself a comfort zone, the thing we are used to. In my case that internal pain stops me from laughing out loud at something funny or for most of the time feeling any kind of real joy for anything. For many years and up until recently, it held me back.

When we are not getting our fill from our creativity, we can allow ourselves to indulge in our weaknesses. There came a point in my life at which I started to say to myself, what have I got to lose? If I'm going to be hurt anyway, why not let others into my world to see my work and expose myself to whatever comes?

I had to learn to accept that not everyone is going to praise and encourage what they see. Whatever your art, your talent is, art is subjective. By putting my work out there, in exposing my talents to the world, I soon found that by doing so it gives a positive adrenaline buzz.

There is an expression …

Opinions are like arseholes; everyone has one but if you get yours out in public you will offend someone!

Being offended is a choice people make. "Ooh I'm offended! That offends me!" No!!

If someone is offended it's because they *choose* to be. I'm sure lots of people will hate what I'm writing and point out all the reasons it's offensive and that's fine, I don't care. If you don't agree then at least you got to think about how it does or rather doesn't work for you. However, understand it does work for me and I think it will be the same for lots of others like me so don't be offended by it otherwise you miss the point. The point I'm making is many people are different to you and they have a right to be. They are just as valid as you and me and their beliefs, views and opinions are also just as valid as yours and mine are, even if they are different.

As humans we all need to learn to replace judgment with curiosity, then perhaps we would understand each other better.

The secret for us NUTs is that we need to take the praise and encouragement, but we also need to allow ourselves to take the negative less to heart and for us NUTs that can be hard.

If I said to you "I hate your yellow hat" and you didn't have a yellow hat, what would you think?

If you do not have a yellow hat, chances are you'd laugh at me. You'd think, what a stupid thing to say and you wouldn't get offended or hurt because you fundamentally know that what was said was stupid and incorrect. You don't have a yellow hat!

Now understanding that being hurt or offended is a choice, when someone criticises me or my work, I simply say to myself

I'm not going to be offended or hurt because I do not have a yellow hat. What you are saying is stupid and incorrect. My intention is not to ridicule or offend others. Whilst I might think about how or what I'm writing or doing is affecting others, I'm not going to choose to let it take me down, emotionally.

If I said you were extremely overweight, obese even, but I said it in a language you didn't understand and I said it with a beaming smile, chances are you'd react in a positive way towards me wouldn't you? You'd take my comments as a positive; after all I was smiling when I said it, and you didn't understand the words I used.

See, it's not what is said that is the issue, it's how we interpret what is said and the context we assume it's being said in that affects the way we chose to react to it. Imagine if you had understood what I had said but, I was your doctor giving you medical advice. Would you choose to be offended? How about if I was your closest lifelong friend worried about your health. What if I said it as an intervention because I love you? You might be hurt but would you let yourself be offended?

How about if we were good friends and I said it as a joke and you knew it was said as part of a joke and that I didn't really see you as overweight, you might not think the joke was funny, but again would you let yourself be truly offended? The question here is when someone says something, we *choose* to be offended by it. Do we really know what the intention and meaning of that person's words were or are we basing our choice to become offended on our own interpretation?

I ran a course on this subject recently. One of the delegates came to me afterwards and said she didn't like one of the principles I had shared with the group because it was my opinion and not a fact. Clearly, I had touched a nerve with her that had evoked an emotional reaction, so she was quite forceful in her approach. In the past I would have felt hurt, wounded and would have had dwelled on it over several sleepless nights. It may well have stopped me from running anymore courses. Instead, I was able to look beyond her very negative reaction and having said to myself I do not have a yellow hat, I was able to give a good, calm reasoned answer. I had after all told the group that it was my opinion and that it was not backed up by facts.

The point I was making was just that. People have opinions and sometimes they are not supported by the facts however, we have to accept that they have those opinions, and we have to deal with them. People get offended when they shouldn't, but we have to accept that they do, and we have to learn to deal with the situation.

Just telling people they mustn't say something and making laws to silence people doesn't change their opinions, it often actually re-enforces their opinions and beliefs. For example, look at what happened in the US with Trump as President. Much of what he said was not supported by any facts but that didn't stop people believing in his words. When those words were challenged by others it often re-enforced his followers' beliefs that his so-called facts were being manipulated!

As NUTs, to use our talents to make change, we have to learn that we often need to *transform* rather than just *inform*. Clever computer NUTs quite often come up with brilliant new ways of doing things, new programs, saving time and money, making huge efficiencies. However, for these new initiatives to work they have to transform the way others work on a day-to-day basis. Simply informing people how to use a new program doesn't gain buy-in. However good the new system is, it won't work unless we transform the way people work by getting them to see the value in it for themselves and to be willing participants.

Before we can transform a situation, we must first listen to how others feel and understand, what their reasoning is. On reflection, I realised that I had not done this with the group that resulted in the lady having a go at me. Instead, I had just informed the group of my thoughts without first gaining an understanding of how they each felt and what they believed. Yes, I made a mistake, we all do.

Using the Yellow Hat principle, by not allowing myself to be hurt but instead looking for the learning in the situation, I was able to thank this lady for her honesty. I was able to engage in a constructive, enjoyable conversation with her and explain my point further. With reason and facts, I was then able to transform her thinking and we parted on good terms. As a learning point for me, I took away the understanding that in future, when delivering that part of the course, I need to ask the delegates about how they see it. So that I can take their opinions into account.

I was able to turn what had started out as a negative, potentially confrontational exchange, into a positive enjoyable learning experience.

As creatives, we are never going to get away from facing negative situations, but we can learn to control them and turn the negatives into positives.

Before leaving school, as well as doing paper rounds during the week, I worked weekends at a farm. Although I didn't know it at the time, the farmer George, was a multi-millionaire who owned and ran a number of highly successful businesses, he loved farming so chose to be a farmer. That was lucky for me. I think because he liked my work ethic, he took me under his wing and became my sort of unofficial mentor. By listening to me, encouraging me and making me feel valued, he instilled some self-worth and confidence in me. He was also full of wise words, many of which I remember and use to this day. He once said to me, "How you react and respond to situations is in your control. The best helping hand is on the end of your own arm."

A friend once had a young man working for him who had been diagnosed as being autistic. He was a great worker, very loyal, such a nice young man who found it very hard, if not impossible to tell lies. The young man's wife was a delight. She supported and encouraged him and made sure he was always smart and on time. Now normally you could set your watch by him as he was never late. One day he was not just late, but very late. My friend was quite worried and when the young man did eventually turn up, my friend let his frustration get the better of him. Seeing my friend's frustrated face the boy cowered in front of him. "Where the hell you have been?!" my friend shouted. "I'm so sorry" the young man said, "I got carried away, my wife and I were trying to make a baby."

How could my friend argue with that? After all, for us NUTs how refreshing would it be if only we could be so honest with people without them taking offence or thinking we were trying to be superior or taking the rise out of them? My friend told me afterwards his reaction was inappropriate. He should have listened before jumping to a conclusion. Had he done so he might have laughed, as you probably just did.

Talking about the autistic spectrum let's get my pet hate out of the way. Many years ago, when I was a young man, I worked with a band whose bass player had a colostomy bag, a stoma. He was, and still is, a great bass player and is also a good friend. We were on the way to a gig in the van and had been on the road for some considerable time and so he needed to stop and empty his bag. Like many of us NUTs, I do tend to care about people and things often more than perhaps I should. Having this caring nature, I said to him, "It must be horrible having to live with that disability."

To my total surprise he turned to me, looked me directly in the eyes, took hold of my hands and said, "Steve, my friend, let me stop you there. When I was a young boy, I was so ill that I just wanted to die. Having the colostomy saved my life and gave me a new life. It was a blessing." He continued, "It's who I am. It's all I know, it can't be fixed, and I don't want it fixed, it's part of me. I'm not disabled I'm just different to you. I just have to operate in this world slightly differently to you. It's not like it's something wrong with me it's just we are different, and this is just part of my difference to you."

As you can imagine I felt so stupid, mortified even that I had not seen how obvious that was. That day I learnt a huge lesson. We are all different, most of us NUTs have challenges of one sort or another but it's who we are. We just need to operate slightly differently in this world and that is why to this day I hate 'labels'.

When people say, "Oh you have this or that condition." As though it is something wrong with you, they are wrong, it's who we are, it's all we know. I am dyslexic. It affects my reading and my writing; it gives me challenges with Maths and my memory for certain things like names is not as good as many others. However, I don't see it as though I *have dyslexia*, like it's some sort of illness or something that is wrong with me.

By all means use the word dyslexic to describe me if that helps you better understand me but, it's who I am, and it's all I know. I just need to make certain adjustments to best operate in this world and my genius in other things more than compensates for it. Whilst in some areas I'm not as good as others, in other ways, like so many of us NUTs we have talents that outshine so many others.

I believe that as NUTs our genius most often comes from the very things that make us different. Rather like someone who is blind but has incredible hearing and sense of smell and touch or someone who is unable to communicate verbally and is very introverted but is a genius with Maths and IT.

The brilliant, animated video called *"Why the dyslexic brain is misunderstood"* researched by Rajaa Elidrissi talks about how in 2001 a major study was carried out to compare the way people diagnosed as being dyslexic operated in comparison with the general population.

You may have seen what are referred to as *Impossible Drawings*. Drawings of what looks like a staircase that keeps going up even though it goes round and round in a circle. Or a box that has sides that makes it impossible to actually exist. There are loads of these *Impossible Drawings*. They are called impossible because in reality, it would be impossible to make them. They are illusions and many of them are hard to see as impossible however, the outcome of this study was to conclusively show that those diagnosed as being dyslexic were much faster than the average person in identifying the impossible drawings against drawings that were similar but are possible to make. This adds to the many researchers who now link dyslexia with a talent for visual-spatial ability, i.e. the ability to process the whole image rather than as most do, looking at it, part by part.

This study was just one of many which have highlighted something most dyslexic people already know, whilst they have challenges with for example reading and writing, they also have enhanced abilities in other areas. In most cases, these tend to be in the way dyslexic people can see the whole picture, even often visualising it.

Many dyslexic architects for instance say they can visualise a building in their mind rather like a 3D model and can even rotate that image to see it from different angles.

I was once described as having a *planet brain*. A brain that could see all the possibilities and how they link together. That's exactly how I do see things, even challenges. I was surprised to find out most people don't see things the way I do, and that instead have more of a tunnel vision, only seeing one thing at a time and having a challenge linking things together.

In terms of evolution our brains have no specific region for reading like there is for sleeping or engaging our fear response. Reading is a human invention that is only six thousand years old.

Whilst we still have so much to learn about our brains, reading is an area that is now mostly understood. Brain scans show that as we learn to read, the average brain develops areas, mostly in the left hemisphere, that then link together so that a fluent reader can process a word in milli-seconds. We even have names for each of these regions. We know what each of these functions are and can draw a map of how they link together. The pathways that connect each region we call white matter, neural pathways. In the dyslexic brain however, these regions and neural pathways are different, and the brains right hemisphere areas are far more active.

Dyslexia has no bearing on someone's intelligence. Every dyslexic person is different. Typical challenges can include retrieving mathematical facts, grammar and the working memory or reading numbers. Sometimes dyslexic people panic as words on pages seem to float. They find others have already finished an exam whilst they are still reading the questions because they read much slower. However, the facts seem clear, dyslexic people are compensated by enhanced abilities in other areas such as high-level reasoning, problem-solving, special processing, episodic memory and creativity. Many dyslexic people can make associations and link things that to most people do not seem to be relevant. They can make great detectives. Enhanced, very detailed memory is another trait where often someone can draw a detailed picture from something seen years ago. Many can conjure up and visualise music or art even hearing it and seeing it before they create it.

The science world is now starting to understand that, as the human race is developing, we are evolving to have different brain structures that complement each other. The current trend to see one person as correct and others as having some condition or disability that needs to be fixed needs to be addressed. We should understand and celebrate our differences and use them collectively towards the common good.

As a NUT remember you are part of only 2% of the population and the world is therefore constructed at the moment, around the huge majority whose lives revolve around watching and talking about soaps on the TV, the weather and how much they had to drink last night.

Fact. Most people spend more money each year on toilet rolls than they do on self-improvement books, videos etc.

It just goes to show what they think is most important! Part of my personal development, to keep me focused on my mission, has been to every day make time to feed my brain, to watch a video or do something to help improve my mind and my mindset.

Let us look further at this thing, what is normal. Just imagine, if the vast majority of people were in wheelchairs. Do you think the "normal" way our doors, pavements, the ways cars are designed, and the way shops are organised would be as they are?

What about if, the vast majority of people were deep-thinking fact-based introverts with little or no empathy for others as some of us NUTs are? What would most of the programmes on TV be like?

This majority controlling the norm also applies to those who hold the majority of wealth; We know this as the 80/20 rule or the Pareto principle. As Vilfredo Pareto [an Italian economist and sociologist who is known for his theory on mass and elite interaction and also his application of mathematics to economic analysis.] discovered, roughly 80% of land and wealth is owned by just 20% of people. This principle occurs time and time again in society, even with decisions being made on what is *normal* and how we should live. So, on the one hand we have society and its norms being based on how its seen to be easiest and best for the vast majority of people. On the other hand, most of our decision makers are making the rules for that majority based, most often, on their own perceptions and self-interest.

No wonder us NUTs often find it hard to conform and are seen and treated as oddballs or renegades.

Before I go on, I do want to say that yes, I agree, some of us NUTs need to take medication so we can operate in this world. It's just an adjustment. It doesn't make someone a lesser person, nor does it make us lesser people or of any less value if we can't do things others can. You are still just as valuable; you are still just as worthy.

NUTs come in all shapes and sizes. Different skin colours, religions, sexual orientations and upbringings. Some of us have challenges with our mental health, some physical and some emotional but even if we don't realise it yet, we are all geniuses in some way or another.

Our brains are very clever, so very clever that whilst we now know a lot about how they work and what they do, we still have no idea of what our brains are truly capable of. What we do know however is that our brains are rather like massive computers.

Very clever NUTs have now been able to measure the numbers of receptors going to our brains from our senses, our eyes, our taste, our touch, our sense of smell and what we hear. What they have found is that the more we are on, what we can call The Spectrum, the more receptors we have going to our brains. Just like a computer, if you overload a computer with too much information all at once it slows down and functions start to drop off. Some aspects of our brains don't function or work very efficiently but, and here is the genius, with this additional extra data being fed to our brains, we may be different, some of our functions may be affected but the power of our brains can use this extra data to do incredible things. Come up with incredible solutions or art, or music, or understand massively complicated stuff.

Did you know that some NUTs can remember and recall at will every minute of their adult lives? They can describe in detail where they were at any given moment in time and can describe their surroundings and tell you what they and others around them were doing at that very moment?

One of the most popular 1970's sit coms was a TV programme called Taxi. The Hollywood actress and star of the show was a lady called Marilu Henner and she became a huge Hollywood A-lister. But today she is far better known as one of only 10 people in the world, proven beyond doubt, to be able to remember everything. Yes everything. She can remember her whole life. Ask her about a day, any day and straight away she will tell you what day of the week it was, what the world and local news was on that day, what the weather was like and exactly what she was doing, who she was doing it with, what she and they were wearing, what they ate and she can tell you exactly to the minute when each of these things happened. Don't believe me? Look her up!

Because she was so well-known and her life was filmed, photographed, and documented by the press, researchers have been able to fact check her memories. On YouTube there is a 60-minute Australian documentary which features her and others with this talent called "People who remember every minute of their life". These people say their brains work like a Google search, ask them a question and, in their minds, up pops the answer and all the details to go with it.

Having now done MRI brain scans on people with this gift, scientists have discovered something amazing. The common denominator between them is that a part of their brains called the Caudate Nucleus is, in all of them, enormous.

As a human being you are amazing even if your talent is, as yet, hidden and unseen. Everyone is different; everyone's brain is slightly different. You may not have total memory recall or an obvious recognised talent, but you are incredible, you do have a gift.

If someone says their child is disabled or has a challenge, I always ask, "Do you know what their genius is"? Invariably their eyes light up because they realise you understand and see the value in their loved one and not the disability that others can only see.

We have another similarity to a computer. We are programmable. What we feed into our brains is who we will become. We program ourselves by what we read, what we listen to and the environment we put ourselves in. During our awake periods, our conscious brain takes in information from our senses, what we see, touch, smell and hear. Most of us think in pictures, our senses build up what are rather like digital photos and movies of our world and our experiences. This is why we are able to close our eyes and conjure up images in our minds.

When we sleep our subconscious brain, which is rather like the most incredible massive memory bank, opens up and the flow of the day's data is sent from our conscious mind to our subconscious. That's why we dream. It's the pictures and information flowing from our conscious short-term memory to our subconscious. Our brain is cleverly sorting out where the data should be stored along with other similar information and experiences.

Your subconscious mind is incredible, it never sleeps, and that's why you don't die when you are asleep. It keeps your body working, your heart pumping and is still listening ready to wake you up if it detects danger such as a loud noise.

Think about it, I bet if you drive a car you will have had a time when you are driving along a road you have done a number of times before and you are away with the fairies, thinking about something completely different to driving but then something happens and it's like you sort of wake up and say to yourself where am I? Odd, if you think about it, your subconscious was perfectly safely driving the car whilst your conscious mind was on other things.

When you learn to play a musical instrument, you train your subconscious to play the instrument whilst your conscious brain is reading the music and you're reading well ahead of what you're playing.

When you get into a book and you can almost see yourself in the story, chances are you're dreaming up subconscious pictures in your mind from the words you are consciously reading.

When a tennis player or sports person starts hitting those amazing, incredible shots it's because through practice and learning, they have trained their brains so well, that they are able to switch over so that their subconscious is fully in control of their actions.

That's why when we try to consciously think about doing something we are rarely as good as we can be and it's also why if we have trained our subconscious brain to believe we are no good at something or are frightened by something that, however rational our conscious mind might be about the situation, we find it so very hard to do the task or deal with the situation.

One of the world's tennis greats Novak Djokovic talks in interviews about the difference between good players and great players and how much mental strength plays such a part.

He says, *"There are lots of players with good shots but not many with good shots and mental strength. The strength, to have faith in yourself and not give up, even when things aren't going your way. It's not what happens to you or the experiences you encounter but how you live through them, how you deal with them mentally." He goes onto say, before a match, you have to tell yourself to switch off from what is going on around you and just be present, remind yourself that you are there for a reason."*

He also says, *"The harder the moment you are in, the more you have to remind yourself to talk to yourself, to consciously breath and stop the negative thoughts." He goes on to say the experience of being in a difficult situation so many times before in his career helps each time with the next one, helps to face the adversity, the distractions, the what ifs and fears and so forth.*

He continues, *"I think everyone goes through that process and I used to think it was bad, trying to ignore it or shut it down but the major transformation for me, in a positive way, was when I started to acknowledge it and accept it as part of me, my ego was there, my fears are there. It was how then I transform that into positive fuel and to do that I focus on enjoying the moment and being present. It's not easy but I realised no one else can do it for you; you have to face these things yourself."*

There is a well-known saying …

"Genius borders on insanity."

For many of us NUTs, we are able to access our subconscious when we are awake. For the vast majority of people, if they have a challenge and they sleep on it, chances are when they awake, their subconscious will have brilliantly analysed the data and provided their conscious waking mind with a solution.

Those of us, who can access our subconscious at will, when we are awake therefore have a superpower. We are able to tap directly into the *genius of our minds* but, that can also pose us a challenge. As most of us think in pictures, sometimes we do not know the difference between reality and our dream state. We can see things and scenarios that are not there, and we can believe we have done things or had experiences that actually we haven't in real life.

This is exacerbated further by the fact that, as human beings, we have evolved and developed a very clever way of making decisions quickly. These short cuts to decision making are needed, otherwise with all the data constantly coming to us and the massive amount we hold in our memory banks, we would never make decisions. We would be spending all our time analysing and processing information. Our lives are full of decisions to be made every second of every day. Everything from, "Do I scratch that itch?" to "Shall I eat?" or "Where shall I go on holiday?" Almost everything is a calculated decision.

So, to enable us all to function in this world and make decisions we have developed these shortcuts which we call feelings.

In the late 1800's a railway worker, Phineas Gage, was working near where a huge explosion happened. The explosion sent a steel rod through his left cheek and out of the top of his head destroying part of his brain, the Ventromedial Prefrontal Cortex to be exact. He fell to the ground. Everyone assumed he was dead but surprisingly he recovered. But, from then on, he was unable to control his emotions or make rational decisions. Now fast forward to 1994 when the eminent neuroscientist Antonio Damasio removed that same area of the brain from one of his patients who had a brain tumour. He saved the patient's life but, as with Phineas Gage, the patient was then unable to control emotions or make rational decisions. After this experience Damasio went on to write the seminal work Descartes' Error, explaining how interlinked our decisions are to our emotions. How we cannot make decisions without using emotions as a short cut to all the information and data that our brains are processing.

It's why when we make decisions, we often say that it doesn't *feel right* or even though the facts would suggest we should do something, we say *my heart is not in it* or *it's a gut reaction.*

Truth is, our hearts have no feelings, it's all in that portion of our brains that make shortcuts to our decision-making process and how we feel about things.

Let's clarify a couple of things: Firstly, whilst most of us NUTs think in pictures, not all of us do. Scientists have described a condition, Aphantasia, in which some people are totally unable to visualise mental images and instead think in words, maths and sometimes smells. If that describes you, fear not, that's normal as well, just different. Chances are you might find it hard to look others in the eye or to recognise people by their faces. We are all different but still just as valid and valuable as each other.

The other thing is that us NUTs tend to either have heightened feelings and emotions. So the way we react and act at times can seem extreme, or, we use more data and less feelings than the average person to drive how we operate. Because of this we can come across as lacking empathy and understanding other people's feelings and what affects them.

The one commonality we do share however, with all other human beings is, we are all products of what we have fed our own brains. In the future we will become the person that we now program ourselves to be. Remember, earlier I said if you want to be an alcoholic go to the pub and hang about with alcoholics. If you want to be a drug addict, go hang about with drug addicts. Therefore, if you want to overcome challenges and become the best you, if you want to be successful and learn to deal with stuff, then feed your brain, on a daily basis, with good stuff.

By stuff I mean books, videos, podcasts and associate with the right people. Just like learning to drive or learning a musical instrument or most anything in life, we train our brains to be who we are. As our feelings are in truth the way we operate to make decisions, the more we train our brains with the right stuff, the more our feelings will take shape, giving us confidence. By doing this we feel better about ourselves, happier, less stressed and in turn you will find you have more self-worth and feel more valued.

I know. It's easy to say but it can be hard to do. As NUTs, we often find it easier to do the opposite. To lock ourselves away, not associate with others and try to take our minds off stuff by watching pointless films or playing computer games. Shutting ourselves off from the outside world rather than facing it. We tell ourselves we won't upset others and as we worry about what others think of us and how they will judge us, it seems the solution but it's not. It's not the way to deal with stuff. Staying up all night so you get so tired you eventually have to fall asleep is not helpful. Drink, drugs, self-harm or abuse is a distraction and won't solve anything. In fact, this behaviour will always make things worse. Bad habits will program your brain to make how you feel about yourself worse and worse in an ever-decreasing spiral.

So, what do you do?

Well, first as you've got this far reading this, well done you're already doing it. As you are reading this, that tells me you are a winner, doing something to improve your mind and knowledge. So your feelings can help you make better decisions going forward.

The Solution:

1. **Switch off the crap.** Make yourself read, watch and do positive stuff, self-help stuff every day. Little and often.

2. **Face your fears**. What I mean is make yourself do some of the things you are avoiding. Yes, when you do you will most likely have a physical reaction. It might make you feel sick, ill, you might shake, or stiffen up, you might even throw up and that's normal. It's the fight or flight reaction. Just like going on stage. In the first-place people will often feel or can even be sick before they walk out on stage but, by making yourself do it and saying to yourself I can handle the physical reaction, eventually the physical reaction will subside and your fear will turn into excitement, it's all adrenaline. As creatives we often take adrenaline as fight or flight thinking it's an instruction not to do something when

in fact once we learn to control it, it becomes the excitement that drives us to do more.

Remember how full of fear you were when you first started to learn to drive or to ride a bike? Then how great you felt when you had mastered it. How, most likely you were so excited about it, you couldn't wait to get out on the road and travel around with your newfound talent.

Can you recall how hard it was to learn to read or write when you were little? Now you devour books, now that you've trained your brain to overcome the challenge.

CHAPTER 4

THE POWER OF A WORD

Because of who you are, most likely you'll find others come to you to solve their 'problems.' But here is the thing, what is the difference between a problem and a challenge?

Think about it. Isn't it just the way we look at a situation? A mindset? Most people see 'problems' as something hard or impossible to overcome. As NUTs we have the ability to see all problems as just another challenge. Isn't it the case that we see a challenge as just an obstacle to be overcome?

When Covid put the world into lockdown and I could no longer travel as I had been doing, no one could come to my recording studio, and I couldn't perform as a musician or work with people face to face. I had to re-think how I could operate. I had previously offered some business mentoring, so I decided to grow that side of my income. I soon found myself in high demand as a listening ear via the internet using Zoom and Teams.

At first everyone seemed to be coming to me with their problems, "Oh I can't do this, and I can't do that."

To be honest it was becoming an irritation. Then I read a book called *"Get off your But"* by Dr Sean Stevenson. It inspired me. I started telling people that if they came to me with a problem, I would not speak to them. However, if they came to me with a challenge and hopefully how they thought the challenge could be overcome then I would talk to them about it, as much as they liked. At first people would say I've got a problem and I'd say then I won't talk to you. They would laugh and say, "OK I've got a challenge!" It worked. Simply by changing the word, it started to get people to see problems as challenges they could overcome. It started them on a journey to become solution oriented.

Try it, get rid of the word problem from your vocabulary and always use the word challenge, it helps your mindset and has a profound impact on the way others react and view things.

Let's take this a stage further...

People pay to go on adventure holidays or say something was an adventure. So, what is an adventure?

You might like parachuting out of aeroplanes or bungee jumping. Perhaps it's kayaking down the rapids or climbing mountains. Many people like computer adventure games. Others go scuba diving. Lots of people like watching adventure films, or reality TV shows with people subjecting themselves to many different forms of extremes.

Question: What do you do when undertaking an adventure?

Isn't it true that when you go on an adventure, what you are actually doing, is subjecting yourself to a series of challenges to be overcome? In overcoming these challenges, you feel good about yourself, and therefore you get an adrenaline buzz.

It is by overcoming challenges that we build self-worth, self-belief and confidence. Learning and growing by overcoming challenges. It's all a part of the journey we are each on in our lives.

The solution is to stop the 'stinking thinking' and look at problems as challenges, opportunities for us to overcome, grow and learn from.

A problem is just a challenge wrongly perceived. An adventure is something to be enjoyed and to build self-worth from. We are each on our own adventure in life and you are the one behind the wheel of your own destiny.

50

CHAPTER 5
THE MISUNDERSTOOD PERSONALITY

There are so many good books on personality types. Whilst it is an important part of fully understanding who you are, I will for the most part leave that subject to others. However, there is one personality type that I believe is misunderstood, misrepresented by most of society and those personalities are I believe disadvantaged because of it. That personality trait is introversion and many of us NUTs are also introverts.

Probably the best-known teaching and certainly the most used personality type test in the world is that of Myers Briggs. (MBTI). There is no one who is merely a pure introvert or a pure extrovert. We are all on a scale between one and the other. Introversion is effectively the opposite of Extraversion.

An extravert is explained as someone who tends to prefer to communicate by talking and works out ideas by talking them through. They learn best through doing or discussing and have broad interests. An extrovert is seen by society as someone who is loud, often brash, highly sociable and expressive and will willingly take initiative in work and relationships. Very strong extraverts can come across as show-offs eager to perform to a crowd.

Introverts on the other hand are characterised as people who live more in their own inner world and prefer to communicate in writing. They work out ideas by reflecting on them and learn best therefore by reflection, and mental practice. Introverts tend to focus in-depth on their interests and are private, quiet and contained people. Often seen as people who only take the initiative when the situation or issue is very important to them. They can also come across as uncomfortable in doing so. Most introverts do their best work and are at their creative best when they are on their own, surrounded by peace and quiet. Strong introverts can come across as unsociable and can get branded as loners.

Chances are you can see yourself in aspects of both personality traits, that's normal. We are all a mix of the two but, you will probably see yourself more one side than the other, possibly very much more as an introvert or an extravert.

Let's be clear, one is not in any way better than the other and it doesn't matter what mix of the two you have. It is true to say that society favours those who tend to be more extrovert. When it comes to schooling, employment and society as a whole, it tends to favour and reward extravert activity. Because of it this, those of us who are strong introverts can think we must have something wrong with us.

For a strong introvert, even the mandatory use of a camera on a zoom meeting is challenging, and in so many ways introverts are compelled to try to act like extroverts.

Over time, as introverts, we tend to teach ourselves to hide our introversion and even though it is not our natural state we make ourselves act like extroverts. This is because it doesn't take long for us to learn that those who have the loudest voices and push themselves forward are seen by society as having the 'best' ideas. They are also seen as the natural leaders when in fact, many of the cleverest people around us are introverts. Many, many exceptional leaders are and have been introverts like, Albert Einstein, Abraham Lincoln, Rosa Parks, Mahatma Gandhi, Sir Isaac Newton, Eleanor Roosevelt, and Charles Darwin.

At school, Nellie sat at the very back of the class. She was perceived by her peers and the teachers as shy. She didn't make friends easily and wasn't part of the in-crowd. Instead, Nellie quietly got on with her work. She took her work extremely seriously and put effort into all of her subjects. Nellie was, most often, top of her class for the work she did. Unfortunately, she suffered the taunts of others being called a swot and a nerd. Nellie dressed for comfort and saw the short skirts, excessive make up and the flirting of others as provocative. To Nellie these were the traits of tarts that needed to take everything more seriously.

Nellie had a nickname, "Smelly Nellie" it really hurt. Especially as she was fastidious about her cleanliness. However, she never let on how much these taunts would hurt her and, just as she always did, kept her hurt to herself.

It was parents evening; Nellie was super-proud of all the work she had done that term, and the exam results she had obtained. Both her parents would be at the school and would meet her head of year for the first time to discuss her progress. When their time came and she went with them to the form room, she knew for once she would get the praise she deserved and so desperately longed for.

Nellie's form teacher greeted them, "Welcome you must be Nellie's parents do sit down and Nellie you sit here." The form teacher opened her report book which had comments in it from all her other teachers in it too. "Let's see" she said, "Ah yes well Nellie has as always done exceptional work, but we are concerned."

Even though her parents were with her, it was as though to the teacher Nellie was invisible. Her form teacher was talking about her as though she wasn't even in the room.

"The fact is, Nellie really doesn't participate very much. She needs to come out of herself and be more assertive and join in more. It's a common comment from all of her teachers, I'm afraid. Nellie really needs to make friends and speak up more. Rather like Jules does, Jules was the lead in the school play this term!" The teacher told Nellie's parents proudly.

"WHAT?!" In her head Nellie was screaming, "Nothing about how great my work is, nothing about how I'm bullied, somehow that's all MY fault?! You want me to be more like Jules who doesn't do her homework, turns up late, destroys and ruins everything she touches, smokes and treats me like shit! I hate you!" Nellie seethed inwardly.

No one, including her parents, could understand why for the rest of her schooling Nellie was so desperately depressed. She never spoke up. Her work remained unfinished, she flunked her exams, and she even allowed the advances of the boys for some momentary affection. When Nellie left school, she took an easy job in a chip shop rather than going to Uni to pursue the career as a doctor as she had initially set as her heart on. Instead, she dressed to shock people.

However, encouraged by her parents she had counselling, 'to sort out what was wrong with her.' The counselling did help a bit, or so she thought. It re-enforced her belief that she needed to change and be more of an extrovert so for the few years she really did try to be more sociable, outgoing and "normal." But for Nellie it was just exhausting.

At her funeral Nellie was described as *troubled,* she was 21.

This sadly is the story of so many misunderstood introvert personalities but, the science is clear. The world needs to understand that the balance we each have between extroversion and introversion is a chemical one. Introversion is not a social hindrance it's an attribute. It's who we are! It is indeed how we are. It's not something wrong with us or that needs to be changed or modified. We don't need to be more outgoing or sociable. Also, it has a negative physical effect on us if we make ourselves try to be someone who we are not.

Scott Barry Kaufman of the Imagination Institute explained how the extravert and introvert brain responds differently to the dopamine reward system. The chemical dopamine is a neurotransmitter that rewards behaviours and encourages you to repeat them again. But it's not the only chemical. He explains ....

An extravert brain is motivated by social stimuli or rewards like food and social status. When faced with these rewards or the expectation of these rewards, an extravert's brain experiences increased neurological activity caused by increased Dopamine. This is pleasant to them and motivates an extravert to receive more social stimuli and therefore more dopamine.

The other chemical that drives behaviour is Azido Choline, a slow releasing neurotransmitter from the Parenthetic Nervous System.

This chemical is the one that introverts thrive on. An introvert has a totally different experience to an extravert. When their brain receives increased Dopamine, they get easily overwhelmed by it. This is why strong introverts fizzle out in social environments. With too much stimulation introverts do not thrive they get exhausted.

One theory is that introverts have more Azido Choline receptors and extroverts have more Dopamine receptors. Even if this is not yet proven, it is the case that how much you are an extrovert, or an introvert is in effect down to the type of chemical stimulus that your brain is geared towards. It is also the primary reason someone may prefer a quiet evening at home rather than being at a party and why so many great leaders and creatives are introverts and therefore described as deep thinkers.

58

CHAPTER 6
WHY WE CAN'T THINK IN NEGATIVES

When I was at middle school, I remember very well being thrown out of my science class. I think my smugness had at last exacerbated Mr French my science teacher.

He had a sealed glass tank with a pipe coming from it to a pump that sucked the air out. Mr French would demonstrate how he could make plastic bottles inside explode due to the difference in air pressure. Sucking the air out of the tank with nothing inside he exclaimed, "There is nothing inside the tank, that's what nothing is like." Excited by the subject I eagerly put my hand up. "Yes, what is it now Favell?" he mused. "Well Sir, surely that's not nothing?" I told him.

Mr French looked displeased saying, "Favell, come up in front of the class and explain" he taunted, so I did. "Well Sir, it's a vacuum, I can measure the area of it, and I can see through it so I can describe it. Therefore, if I can describe it, it must be something not nothing Sir." At that, the rest of the class laughed. Mr French threw me out of the classroom and into the corridor. I heard him say to the class, "There that's better, that's nothing now!"

Point here is as NUTs, as creatives, part of the 2% club, we have a need to understand things, to challenge stuff and we are not good at accepting things just because that's what we are told. This can, at times, get very annoying for other people.

This happens sometimes with my wife, she is also a creative, a NUT, so sometimes we butt heads trying to make our point to each other. Both talking at the same time, not listening to each other. Instead, hell-bent on doggedly arguing our case until we both get wound up.

I am of course always right! 😊. That's another challenge we can have.

Most of us find it hard to understand how other people seem to be able to just "learn" stuff and regurgitate it for example in exam situations. They will achieve a great grade too when fundamentally they do not completely know how it works. Chances are, having passed the exam, they will then forget it again. Whilst some of us NUTs have a genius memory for facts and figures and therefore are actually brilliant at exams. Other NUTs like me are frankly rather rubbish at them. I know I'm not good at exams and tests because I have a head full of creativity.

For me everything has to be real. Actual real-life stuff and situations I can relate to and therefore work the answers out to. The thing is, I'm pretty brilliant at working stuff out and coming up with solutions, even to things I struggle with. However, in the classroom, subjects like Maths for example I need to do it my own way and I have no capacity for remembering other stuff like equations.

In a test, the way I question everything, even if I think I know the answer, makes me question my own answers to the point that I talk myself out of the answer. This in turn gives me anxiety.

For that reason, I absolutely hate quizzes and always have done. To be honest I would rather poke pins in my eyes than be part of a quiz team. I know others like me, who for the same reason, feel this way about joining in other activities like role play or public speaking. Both of these things, I'm perfectly comfortable doing.

As NUTs we do tend to try to please others. We often get *volunteered* to do the very things we hate and then endure it to please others. Silly thing is we can do this too well, pretending to like something so that others think we enjoy it. Therefore, they keep putting us in that situation and, as we are NUTs, we normally do a good job at whatever we are asked. Therefore, we are our own worst enemies!

I love my wife to bits. In the past she organised things for us to do because she thought I would love it. Until we had an honest discussion only quite recently, and I was open and honest about not liking being volunteered to join a quiz team, she literally had no idea.

After so many years together, why hadn't I told her that sooner you ask? I should have done, but she did it with a good heart and I'm a NUT, so I didn't want to offend or upset her. Plus, as a NUT, I do find it hard to make friends and fit in. Like so many other NUTs, I go along with stuff because I want to be seen as perfect. I love my wife; I want to be her perfect husband.

Perfect is a challenge for us. Most of us have this psychological principle of, 'It has to be perfect, or I'll bin it.' At school, if homework wasn't perfect in my eyes, I would probably not submit it. As a NUT if we don't think we can be the best at something we may not even try. This principle shows up particularly with the things us NUTs create. How often have you thrown away your work or hidden it from others because you have not considered it to be perfect? Are you actually afraid it may not be judged as perfect by others?

How often have you watched others put stuff out there, and witnessed them getting praise and money for it, when you know you could have done it far better?

Why do we indulge in this negative behaviour?

At some point I bet you have listened back to something you have recorded or read something you have written, or you have looked with fresh eyes at something you have drawn or painted. It might be a challenge you have solved or an innovative idea. Something you had put away into the back of a drawer some time ago. I bet when you revisited it you were actually rather surprised at how good it actually is. Sadly, at the time of its creation, your negativity made you hide it away.

Did you know? The odd thing is the human brain is not actually capable of thinking in negatives.

Don't believe me? Then I'll prove it!

Don't think of an Elephant!

Let's try another, *don't* think of a bus.

Do not imagine a cat.

When we try to think of a negative, we can't but instead we do the exact opposite. Tell a child not to do something and you implant the seed that encourages them to do that very thing. Tell an adult not to read that book and the chances are that having planted the seed and made them think of it, curiosity and devilment will make them read it. If you had not mentioned reading that particular book, they would never have considered doing so. Trying to tell yourself not to do something is exactly the same, it's all part of 'stinking thinking'.

If you say to yourself, "Do not do this!" you will evoke the very image that will push you towards doing it. When you say to yourself, "I am not going to worry about something", you evoke the idea that you should worry. By doing that, you are actually telling yourself that this something to worry about, an issue to stress over!

That's why we talk about always being positive and using 'positive affirmations.' Always saying to yourself, *I can, I will, I'm going to, I must, I need to, I did it.*

Instead of I'm not going to worry about something, make it instead, "I'm going to make this something into something really good. I'm going to sort this something out."

Yes, it's normal, when you make a positive affirmation, you may have a physical reaction that feels uncomfortable. Just remember, it's your emotional fight or flight mode kicking in. So, fight back, handle the reaction, say to yourself "I can handle this reaction and eventually it will become good adrenaline." Just like the high from the satisfaction you get when you look back at something you have created knowing its brilliant.

Get rid of 'stinking thinking'. Get rid of telling yourself not to do something, instead tell yourself what you are going to do and what you arc going to achieve.

CHAPTER 7

LET'S TALK ABOUT SEX

As NUTs we are capable of incredible highs but also, if we are not careful, incredible lows too. Our highs can often be seen by others as excessive, and our lows can be periods of severe depression.

One minute we are being told to *calm down* or *not to be so hyper* and the next we apparently need to *snap out of it.*

Those that love us and want to encourage us and make us happy will naturally keep doing things that they saw we enjoyed. For instance, at one time we had, what to us, was a phase when we say, for example, collected stamps or we liked going to a particular place. The challenge is, long after we have moved on from that particular phase, when we have done with it, other people will keep buying us stamps and taking us to that very same place. We probably still like stamps and that place but, as creatives, we tend to have short term interests that are, at the time, all absorbing. When we are into a 'thing' we will want to do it 100% and be the very best at it, hungry for knowledge and driven to practice at it. However, as we get bored of things, after a while we need a new stimulus, a new challenge to excite and engage us.

I have been lucky, for the most part, my life has not had long spells without a passion for one thing or another, that's why I learned to play so many different musical instruments. I know lots of NUTs who have had bad depressions and found it very hard to get back on track because they didn't have a project or activity to challenge and excite them, so they completely lost their drive.

For us NUTs this principle can extend to all aspects of our lives including our sex lives. It's partly why I think the best match for a creative is another creative, someone who *gets you*. Who like you, can be an encourager and is happy to try new things.

Some NUTs have a real challenge expressing their feelings, and some with communication in general. We are all different, but we are just as valuable in society. In whatever way we do communicate the ideal partner for a NUT is someone who you should be able to discuss literally anything with. Someone you can tell what you do and don't like without any embarrassment or worries about how they will judge you. The challenge we face is the last bit, the worry about how they will judge us. For that reason, we, most often, don't tell our partners what we would like to try, instead we both go to the quiz with a smile even though secretly neither of us want to and we can both settle for 'vanilla' sex rather than being honest about what would turn us on.

Even if what we would like to try is something simple, that we consider normal, we are afraid that saying what might turn us on and gives us the excitement and adrenaline could be seen as odd or disgusting or over a boundary line for our partner.

This principle doesn't just apply to sex, but also to most other aspects of our lives and especially within our relationships. We may be more of an introvert or an extrovert, but the challenge is the same. As NUTs we tend not to be good about being honest about how it is we truly feel.

Back to the bedroom, or it might be if you were honest and tried things you'd like, a secluded space somewhere in public or tied up or in a phone box or on the beach or play acting or being spanked. You get the idea?

The average person will discover something you like, something that turned you on so from then on, they will always do that thing. But for you for the first few times, as it was different, it was nice. However, let's say it worked the first time they nibbled your ear, but now having their tongue in your lug 'ole every time is actually turning you off. We don't want to offend or put them down so we don't say anything, but these things can become a barrier for us when next sex is proposed.

The answer is of course in the cold light of day, when sex is not on the table just to be honest. Rather than say don't do that, instead say it was nice and suggest at the same time what might be nice to try now. In the same way, stop assuming your partner likes or wants something just because they did appear to in the past. Instead get into the habit of asking them. What would turn you on? How would you feel about doing this or that?

Again, this principle applies to all aspects of our lives. Sometimes what we would like to discuss might seem too personal. A good way of dealing with that is to use the third person approach. Ask how they feel about others doing this or that and then if their reaction is positive, you can extend it to how do you feel about doing it?

Another particularly good way to broach those difficult sex conversations is for you each to write a series of questions. Once you've each written down your answers you can discuss them together.

Example: How would you feel about ....

You could use multiple choice answers such as:

1. No, definitely not!
2. Happy to try.
3. Yes, would love that!

For us NUTs, this can also work for other aspects of our lives. Here's the thing, if your partner loves you, they hopefully love you for who *you* are and the way you are. They love you because you are a NUT, so you will probably be surprised at how open they are to trying new things and experimenting with you.

You will probably find that opening up to them, and sharing your feelings and desires actually strengthens your relationship and as far as sex is concerned you might even find that discussing new possibilities is liberating and exiting for them too.

When I was at middle school my religious education teacher (showing my age!) Mr Shepherd was a NUT. One day he took me to one side, just before I took an exam. "Favell" he said, "You tend to overthink things, trust your instincts they are normally pretty brilliant. So, if you don't know the answers write down the first thing that comes into your head because you will probably be right."

I took his advice and did just that. I failed the exam of course but I did get far more right than I would have otherwise. His advice has stood me in good stead throughout my adult life. We NUTs often have an intuition about things. This is also true in our relationships.

Not every NUT is sexual. It might be that your normal is low or no sex drive and that's fine. We are all individuals but the same applies, talk to your partner and be honest. If they have a need for sex and orgasms, then there are many ways you can help satisfy their needs without having penetrative sex.

What if I think I might be gay or transgender or a lesbian or something else?

Creatives often have challenges with finding their sexual identity. It can be hard to know if a desire to try something new is who you are or if it's because we need to explore boundaries. We tend to overthink things and as emotions are shortcuts we use to make decisions, when a desire pops up it can be a major cause of anxiety. The answer is to go with the flow.

As long as you're not hurting anyone there is no shame in trying things to see what is and isn't a good fit. Often creatives will have relationships just like we do other things. One minute we are on stage singing, next we are learning to sail, and then we are becoming brilliant at something else. No wonder then that to others our relationships can seem like a series of experiments. Eventually, hopefully we find who we are and the person we can't live without. Note, I say can't live without.

As a creative we are likely to be drawn to another creative and we have already established that creatives can be hard to live with. Two creatives living together can be full of adrenaline. I realised after two failed marriages that I wasn't in need of the person I could live with; I was in need of the person I couldn't live without. Fortunately for me I found her.

NB. Red Flag to watch out for

Whilst we can be strong and often come across as having very strong personalities, in my experience, most creatives will be drawn to a strong-willed partner. Someone they can rely on to be their rock, to take care of them, to stand up for them, to *slay their dragons* as my wife puts it. In the bedroom someone to experiment being submissive with and controlled by them and that's normal. But there is a fine line between that and finding yourself in a relationship where your partner is excessively controlling and abusive. Us NUTs sometimes don't see it and indeed can find ourselves in controlled relationships. Relationships where we are always pleasing the other person and apologising for being human.

Please note: if your friends are telling you that you need help, then listen to them as unfortunately some NUTs can also be controlling abusers. If that is you, **You will know you are**. Get help now as these traits never end well. Go see your doctor. Get counselling, find a support network. In the future you will become the person you program yourself from today to become. Start to do something about it now.

Orgasms

Our emotions control so much. If we have convinced ourselves that we should feel guilty, feel shame or that we are unworthy, then our inner brain can and will at times shut down positive emotion. If we start feeling really happy, we can suddenly find it turns to guilt and what felt good now feels horrible, and very wrong. A good example of this is not being able to enjoy orgasms like we should. The build-up is fine; we think it's all going to be good then it's as if someone throws a switch it's just NO!

Our bodies are controlled by chemicals and just like taking some drugs designed to suppress emotions; our minds can release chemicals to do the same. If we have programmed our mind to believe we should not feel or deserve joy, then our body will take that instruction and turn the joy down or even off completely.

The reverse is however also true. If we program our minds to be happy, to have self-worth, to feel valued, to be relaxed and in control, then when we are faced with a negative, possibly hurtful situation, our bodies will give us chemicals to help us feel good about ourselves. It is therefore possible to overcome the very emotions that could otherwise drag us down. These same happy positive conditions will also allow the body to release chemicals so that we can experience physical and emotional highs such as incredibly strong orgasms.

Just like taking drugs, when our bodies release high quantities of chemicals, we can also suffer from withdrawal symptoms. Let's say you had an incredible high, you know one of those over-the-top NUT-type highs. You were out with your mates, a few drinks, lots of stupidity and lots of laughs. Your body was flooded with happy adrenaline. Then you have to come down again. As NUTs we can easily go from one extreme to the other. Now feeling anger, depression, a lack of energy, even sadness. They are all withdrawal symptoms. You might even experience shaking or other physical reactions.

If we get used to getting a low after a high it can seem a good idea to avoid the highs whenever possible thinking this will stop some of the lows and keep us sane, but of course it's another negative trap we fall into.

The art here is to have and enjoy the highs but to learn to control the lows by feeding the brain with good stuff. By always having something as a project or other that you can look forward to and enjoy doing. The good stuff, positive focused action to improve your mind and self-worth will, in time, soften or get rid of any feelings of guilt and self-loathing you might be holding onto. Those negative feelings which can stop us enjoying all that life has to offer.

CHAPTER 8
UNDERSTANDING YOUR TIME MANAGEMENT

Have you noticed when you ask the majority of people what they are thinking about they say, "Nothing, I'm not thinking of anything."

If you're like me, you probably find that hard to believe or understand. That's because a common trait of us NUTs is that our thoughts never stop. We cannot think of nothing in fact, a challenge we have is, we have so much in our minds all the time, that it's hard to know what to concentrate on.

Well, the fact is most people at times can think of nothing. As NUTs the best most of us can do is to use something like for example, yoga or some form of meditation, to clear our minds regularly. Otherwise with our minds sparking new ideas and being always active time management becomes a real issue.

So, if this is you, I've got some remedies that may work.

Number one: stop saying *I don't have the time*. It's a lie! Accept that you control your time so, if you choose to make something a low priority then that's a choice you made. There is a big difference between *I can't,* and *I don't want to,* or *I am making something in my mind more important than that.* Therefore, it's not *I don't have the time*, it's *I choose not to make that a priority*. Be honest with yourself it will help put things into perspective.

Number two: We are easily distracted and try to do far too much all at once, often not being effective with anything, which starts us thinking we are no good. Our art, our creative side goes out of the window and even if we make ourselves try, we just get frustrated because we can't get into the zone. We say our 'creative juices have dried up' or 'I'm just rubbish!'

For me writing this is a perfect example. For months I've been busy working, paying the bills, filling my days with 'stuff' that seemed urgent and I've had no creative urge or energy. Yet here I am on holiday in Greece in the sunshine, relaxed and I just can't stop writing, its literally pouring out of me! As creatives we need the space in our heads to be creative. To be the real us we have to get the right work/life balance, clearly before this holiday I'd let mine slip way out of kilter.

Back to things we can do…

Number three: Emails. Trying to answer emails whilst allowing distractions, such as, your phone pinging messages or other emails popping into your inbox is a big mistake. Turn them all off. Research shows it takes twice as long to answer your emails if you keep stopping to look at other stuff. When you return to what you were doing you have to go over it again to get back on track.

The key here is to focus on one task at a time and turn off all other distractions whilst you're doing that one task.

Number four: If you were making something on a production line, you'd plan what you were going to do and when. It's obvious. First, you'd need to design and cost whatever it is you're making. Then source and order the materials. Then you'd plan and diarise each step of the process so that at the end you would have a finished product, on a known day and time.

So, why is it that as creatives we don't do that with our diaries? Instead, we get up each day with a huge list of stuff to do in our heads and no plan for the week. We don't look at what we need to do or plan when and how we will do it. We then find it hard to prioritise what needs to be done first.

Therefore, use your diary, plan your week. For instance, you might answer your emails every morning between 9 and 10. Then reward yourself with a coffee before doing the next planned task. Every Tuesday at 4pm you might make that the time to call your colleagues to answer their queries or check in with them. They will get used to when you will call which also helps with the overall consistency. That way we don't have to worry about an 'Oh no I've forgotten to do that!' moment.

This has another huge advantage; many of us NUTs need the comfort blanket of a habit-forming routine. By planning our week and diarising activity we can also give ourselves a consistent routine and plan in time for our creativity.

Number five: Get into the habit of doing the 'one thing' every day. We tend to spend most of our time doing what seems most urgent rather than what is most important. So, let's say we need a job. The most important thing that day would be to start applying for jobs Often in our minds we will not have the time because we are doing what we see as most urgent. For example, like getting our perfect CV together. However, that's far less important than getting those applications out there. Be honest with yourself and make a list of the seven most important tasks you need to do each week then, diarise one per day making that the 'one thing', the most important 'one thing' you will definitely do that day.

That way, even if for some reason that's all you manage to get done that day, you have achieved the most important task. You will feel good about yourself, plus you won't wake up, or rather stay awake most of the night, worrying about all the stuff you still have to do.

Number Six: To be creative you need downtime. i.e. Creative time. Time for yourself. Time to relax, to pursue your passions and have a work life balance. Therefore at least one of those seven days in the week, make time for your creativity as the 'one thing' you do that day.

Number seven: There is a saying, 'work expands to fill the time available' and it's so true. It was a phrase coined by Cyril Northcote Parkinson in a 1955 article he wrote for the Economist, which explored the relationship between work and working hours. Later it was featured in his excellent book, Parkinson's Law which, although it was first published in 1958, still has real thought-provoking significance today.

In my own experience I have found that if I give myself a whole week to compose a musical jingle then chances are it will take me the whole week. However, if I give myself just a day, I normally achieve it. This principle seems to work every time. The magic here is that if you set yourself deadlines to achieve tasks you are most likely to save yourself loads of time. Make a deal with yourself. Say I'm going to do that, in that amount of time, then I will reward myself with some 'me time', some creative time.

Number eight: It feels good when we complete a task and physically cross it off a list. Look at your diary each day and make a list of the things you've planned to do that day then cross them off as you do each one. Make sure you have put on the list your 'one thing' for that day so you can do that as a priority even if you don't get all the others done. The added benefit here is that as NUTs we have the tendency to beat ourselves up at the end of the day for not achieving anything, even when we did do stuff. With our crossed off list we can reflect on what we have achieved which feels good and builds our self-worth. Sometimes if life is particularly hard that might be the realisation that we simply survived the day.

One other thing about sorting your time management out. This has an effect on the last section about sex and what turns us on. For many of us NUTs feeling progress is being made, that things are happening, that we are in control of our lives, and we are relaxed is a key ingredient. As my wife once said to me when I asked her, "What would turn you on honey?" she replied, "The front room, finally being decorated!"

CHAPTER 9
TAKING OWNERSHIP

Thinking about being in control, us creatives, more often than not, have a challenge delegating to others. We are generally not good at taking criticism, even though we say we are. After all, when we have done or created something isn't it true that it's as good as it can be? If someone tells us it could be better in some way, doesn't it feel like a personal attack? It's yet another challenge we face. In reality we don't have the time or energy to do everything ourselves, but we often feel like we have to. Saying things like, "No I'll do it!" or "I need to do that." is something I often find myself saying and the truth is on most occasions I don't *need* to do it myself at all. If I let someone else, do it, I'm often surprised how good it is.

Over the past few years I have, however, come to like the saying, 'Why put off until tomorrow what you can get someone else to do today.' After all isn't it better for the task to be done even if you could have done it better or you would have done it a different way? Rather than adding it to the endless list that you will actually never complete. If you did do it, it would probably be at the expense of something far more important, like time for you to be creative? Ownership isn't about you doing everything. It's about using your talents to their best effect.

In the early 70's I worked with a brilliant electronics engineer, a real creative. He designed some of the best, cutting edge electronics for the music industry at that time. Having done this for others he decided to set up his own company and he produced one of the very first electronic drum kits commercially available in the world.

His drums were brilliant. His designs and ideas were innovative, so his business took off with orders flowing in from all over the world. As a design engineer he was one of the very best that was, with his talent, his skill set. As his business grew, more and more he became a manager of people. Managing the company finances and quality control and export and, and, and! You get the idea. Now tied up running the business he had no time for design, so he employed other engineers who were not as good as him. It wasn't long before the quality started to drop. The final blow came when, due to his lack of knowledge, he exported a large shipment of drums to Germany and didn't get paid. He hadn't put the safeguards in place which someone with a talent for export management would probably have seen as obvious.

I'm happy to report that having learned his lesson he did go on to be a huge success. The second time around he stuck at what he was good at, his talent, his skill set, and he gave control to others who had the experience and genius to run the areas of the business that he lacked. This included employing a CEO who he effectively reported to on a day-to-day basis. This enabled him to concentrate on his passion and gift, that of being an innovative design engineer.

Ownership is taking responsibility for your own actions, to recognise our own strengths and weaknesses, to play to our strengths and work with others to complement what we do to achieve any given goal. This means we have to learn to delegate and allow others to work with us. We may not like being told what to do but, if we are not gifted as a leader, then we need to recognise our need to follow the direction of others. We also need to learn to do all we can to understand another's point of view. After all, if someone feels something, even if we disagree, we must recognise that they feel that way for a reason. If we want to change their mind, we need to understand the other person's reasons and what makes them feel and see things the way they do.

The only person in this world we can really change is ourselves. As NUTs if we want to effect change then we must look at how *we* do things and how *we* interact with others.

A mantra for creatives …

If it's to be, it's up to me!

STEVE FAVELL

CHAPTER 10

GETTING OUT FROM UNDER THE CIRCUMSTANCES

It was a particularly cold February night in the cabin when, all alone, Lorna gave birth to her second son. She already had a two-year-old boy, sleeping fitfully in the corner. Dressed in second-hand clothes, with barely enough wood on the fire to keep the three of them warm. The last of the embers were glowing in the grate, the log basket was empty, and it had been hours since Lorna had eaten the last scraps of the rabbit stew. Outside the snow lay thick and the wind howled through the pine trees. As usual Dirk, her so-called husband. was nowhere to be seen. For once she was glad. This was one occasion when she didn't care if he was with his whore further down the side of the mountain. Lorna huddled with her newborn child, praying, hoping so much that now, having two baby boys to look after, he would at last change his ways.

Her prayers were in vain as things got worse. As the brothers grew up, they witnessed their father as an abusive and violent, drug addict. Permanently out of work, unwilling to support his family, or ever to show any affection towards their mother or them. If he got hold of what little money Lorna scraped together, as a result of her taking in washing for the miners, he would spend it on more substances.

Dirk was a bum. Living and growing up in squalor the best memories for the boys were made when he was in prison where, eventually, he died. The boys were brought up by their loving mother and they shared everything. This included all the horrors they and their mother had endured. Aged 16 and 18 both boys left home and for the first time in their lives, set out to make their own individual futures.

It was in the spring, five years later, when Lorna herself also set out to visit each of her sons. Arriving at the prison gates she went inside to see her oldest son. Just like his father he was a drug-taking, violent bum, looking through the glass partition at his gaunt face she asked, what made you like this son? He snapped back, "Ma, what did you expect?" he spat, "What choice did I have under the circumstances but to be like my father."

Visiting her younger son was a completely different story. He didn't take drugs of any kind. In contrast to his brother, he had a lovely wife and happy children. He also had a really good job and a lovely home. For the past four years he had also been supporting his mother. Sitting in the sunshine surrounded by all of the beautiful flowers in his garden she asked, "Son what made you like this? He smiled, "Ma what did you expect?"

What choice did I have under the circumstances. There was no way I was going to be like my father!"

The story reminds me of a young woman who went to a wise man for some advice. She explained how she was trapped. Trapped in her flat, trapped in her relationship and trapped in a job she hated. Then she said it, those very words, "Under the Circumstances."

In that moment the wise man couldn't help himself. "Under the circumstances?!" he said, "What are you doing under there? You don't want to be under there now do you? Get out from under there woman!"

The definition of madness …

Keep doing the same thing and expect different results.

Remember …

If nothing changes, then nothing changes.

My mentor always said, stop being a 'settle for', settling for this and settling for that. The best helping hand is on the end of your own arm! He told me, "If you don't like something then change it!"

For example: If you don't like your flat then find another and move. Treat finding a new flat as a project, work to find a new flat as though it is a job you have to do. If you are presently stuck in a contract so you have to stay for a while, then the project move date is therefore set for when the contract ends. Now you have a plan, something to work towards and to look forward to.

The only person you can change is yourself so change your attitude and what you are doing.

If you feel trapped in a relationship then look at yourself and be honest, are you the problem or the solution?

Take ownership of your situation. Are you indulging in 'stinking thinking?' Are you watching the world go by and moaning about your lot? Or are you making things happen? Ultimately if your relationship is not working then you need an open discussion with your partner to see why and to see if you can fix it. Chances are to fix it you will have to change. Therefore, part of that discussion needs to be how much you are prepared to change and can change. You might say that doesn't sound fair, after all there are two people in this relationship. Fairness is just ego my friend. In any negotiation you need to look for a win, win situation. A situation where both parties come out with a better outcome. It's not about winning and losing. Life isn't fair. If your partner is also prepared to change that's a bonus. Remember the only person we can change is ourselves so, always look to see what *you* can do. If after everything the relationship is not to be then just remember, being single is better than wishing you were.

In your job, if you are feeling unfulfilled, that you are not being stretched or valued, is it because you don't have the right attitude and mindset? Are you enthusiastically and actively engaging? Are you making things happen, giving 100%?

Or is it just not a good fit for you and your talents? If you have challenges with other members of staff, ask yourself, what can I do about it? Ask yourself how can I take ownership and change the situation? There is a great saying …

A friend is a gift we give ourselves.

One of my management sessions most people find hard to put into place is how to manage up. How to manage our managers. The principles for this are the same for building relationships with people we find hard to deal with or relate to.

Step 1 is to find out what their goals and objectives are, how they are measured and what motivates and engages them. Then we can work with them towards their goals and aspirations.

Step 2 is to be the solution not the problem. Imagine if you had several members of staff, most of whom were constantly moaning, but one was always positive and eager to help you, you'd warm to that person, wouldn't you? Chances are the one person who was keen to work with you, you'd start to build a positive relationship with. It's all about taking our eyes off ourselves and putting them onto others.

Step 3 is to give them praise and let them take the praise for things even if it was actually, you that did the good work. Trust me, I know it's hard, but it works miracles and, in time, your effort will be noted by others.

As a creative you need to have a job that stretches you or you will become bored, unengaged, lethargic and demotivated. If your focus is elsewhere and the job is just a means to an end, to earn you cash, to support your creativity. But recognise that. You can still give the job 100% or it will become a chore.

You might think I'm being very heavy handed here. You might be thinking I sound like a bully. Moving forward for us NUTs requires us to constantly evolve. We need to continue to challenge ourselves, to face up to and to fight the fear. To overcome that which holds us back, because it's in our own minds that we put up barriers. We do it to ourselves. If we let ourselves become negative, we become the actual problem in our own lives. As a NUT the problem can be me, but so is the solution. I've learnt that when I find myself under any circumstance which is uncomfortable then, I have to change myself and/or what I am doing.

Ask yourself this question: If I was totally on my own. No phone, TV or any distractions. I was warm, well fed but had no one but myself to talk to for three days, would I be in good company?

If actually you wouldn't like yourself as you are, you have the power to change. Whilst it can be hard, you have the genius to make stuff happen. Stuff most others can't do. Ok yes, you might have challenges that others don't have, it's just a fact but use your talents, the power you have. Set yourself some small steps, things you can see you can do and make them happen, so you feel good about yourself. It will help you to believe you can do the bigger stuff too.

Everything starts with a dream, an idea. The building you are in right now didn't exist until someone had the vision in their head and the drive and determination to make it happen. The chair you sit on, the cup you drink from, every man-made thing starts with an idea, a vision and someone to make it happen. You are in control of you and your life. You can make wonderful things happen for yourself and others, but you will never know what you can achieve unless you try.

So, let's start the work today on the next chapter of your life.

STEVE FAVELL

CHAPTER 11

MAKING YOUR PLAN OF ACTION

As a NUT you are naturally curious, already you find yourself asking Why? Why does that happen? Why does that work that way? Why do I feel this way? But you also have a talent so let's just add one magic word to our Whys that makes all the difference and gives us a plan of action. The word is not!

<u>Why Not?</u>

It's all a state of mind, instead of just saying Why? Add the word not and start by thinking, Why *not?*

Why *not* make that happen?

Why *not* make it work that way?

Why *not* make myself feel good by doing this?

You can make stuff happen. You know this because so many times in the past you have wanted something so much you focused on it and worked at it. You made it happen, didn't you?

The danger is, if we focus on being ill or feeling fear or other negative stuff, we can make that happen too. Therefore, we must make ourselves *always* focus on the positive. Yes, we might still get ill or have something bad happen, but the effects won't be so bad. Even when we are not at 100%, as a NUT, you can still make good stuff happen.

Being dyslexic, getting virtually no grades at school, and not being a university graduate, you'd think I had no chance of getting a job on the senior team at an FE College. Especially as I'd never worked at one or at any school for that matter. However, when a job came up, running a large business department for an FE College with a brief to grow the College Employment Engagement, I just said to myself why not? What have I got to lose by trying?

As I drove into the campus that first day, having got the job, I asked myself, how the hell did I get to be doing this? From a standing start with virtually no employer engagement at all? In the first year, simply by applying my NUT logic, after all I had no academic qualifications or learning to do the job, my department increased the College income by more than £1.5 million! Furthermore, we were described by Ofsted as being 'one of the best employer engagement Colleges in the country.' Now, don't get me wrong, this wasn't rocket science. I'm not that clever. As a NUT you could have done the same job as me in the same situation.

It was just doing what you and I would see as obvious. It's also why we find other people hard to understand and frustrating at times. As a creative, you will see the wider picture. You would say things like, 'If you did this over here, then that would make that happen. In turn that would do that so, it would therefore change that, and therefore the challenge would be solved.'

You have the ability to see how things link together and affect each other. It's hard to understand we don't all do this, but most people don't. That's why people come to you with their problems and, most often, I bet you come up with the perfect solution. A solution which to you seems obvious. So obvious that it makes you wonder why they can't see it.

The big message here is don't underestimate your abilities.

STEVE FAVELL

CHAPTER 12
DESIGNING YOUR FUTURE

Time to talk about reverse engineering. If we are going to make something, we first decide what it is that we are going to make and what purpose it serves. Having established what it is, we would work backwards to come up with what it will be made of. We look too at how we will get the materials and eventually what the steps are we will need to take to create a finished product. The principle is simple and obvious, we decide what we want then we reverse engineer it.

Even a car journey is planned, reverse engineered; we have a destination we want to go to, so we plan our route and work out a time frame. We probably have set ourselves a time to leave and we check to make sure we have with us what we need for the journey. We may encounter obstacles or diversions and we may be delayed so we don't arrive on time. But unless we give up and go home, we will always find a way to get there.

By metaphorically planning the journey I never get lost. Oh yes, at times I go off track, drive down roads I don't recognise, and I didn't intend to. However, if I know where I started from and where I'm going to, I can, at any point, ask myself where am I now? All I have to do is eventually work out how to get back on track to end up at my destination. I'm not lost, I just made an unexpected detour, and it perhaps took me longer than I planned, but that's life. It is the same with whatever we do.

Planning is a fundamental task we do every day, all the time. We do it with travel journeys, what we are going to buy or build, what we are going to wear but other than the occasional holiday or purchase, most of us don't do this with our lives. Instead, we wake up each day with no particular plan, other than to do that which seems most urgent. Is it then any wonder when we don't feel in control of our lives? The challenge with designing our lives is often we don't actually know what we do want. As a creative, one of our biggest challenges is, we tend to be good at so much. It's hard to decide which direction to go in. If *you* don't know which direction to go in or what *you* want in life, then *you* need to get out and try stuff.

As a young boy I decided I wanted a Mercedes car, I don't know why, I'm not really into cars but it seemed a big enough goal to be set as a milestone in my life, so it was a major incentive in everything I did.

I had a picture of a luxury model on my wall opposite my bed. It was the last thing I saw before I went to sleep and the first thing I saw when I woke up each morning. Anytime I drove past one in my rusty old Ford Anglia I used to say, "I'll have one of those one day." Comes the day I finally had the hard-earnt cash in my bank. I went along to the car showroom with my cheque book in hand. I walked into my local dealership, full of excitement and anticipation. I was so excited I was actually shaking as I pulled open the showroom door. The salesman took me to a gleaming, new, top of the range model and opened the door so I could sit in it and, in his words, "Smell the real leather interior." I was, by this point, almost breathless with anticipation as I got inside. Then, devastation! All my energy drained out of my body, I felt the blood drain from my head, and I felt weak and physically sick as I felt my world collapse around me. Why? I had been working towards this goal for years. It was my dream; I had reached my goal, and I could afford it. But being short, I literally couldn't see over the bonnet! It hadn't occurred to me that I wouldn't be able to sit in the seat and see over the bonnet without a cushion and if you have ever tried to drive a car that you cannot see over the bonnet you would understand. Imagine the indignity of resorting to sitting on a cushion in your brand-new Mercedes!!

Yes, in hindsight it is funny but, at the time, it honestly wasn't. That realisation of what I had worked so hard for, slipping away from me in a flash. Realising it literally wasn't a good fit for me now that I'd finally achieved it. I was genuinely devastated, and it took me weeks to recover. I learned the hard way. They do say be careful what you wish for as you just might get it.

The real lesson I learned was that I should have touched, smelt and sat in the car before I set my mind on it as a goal. If your dream is a new home, go look at houses to see what really is a good fit. If it's a new career do some voluntary or part-time work doing that very job so you can establish if it excites you and is what you expect it to be. The point here is, if you don't know which direction to go in or what you want in life, then you need to get out and 'dream-build', try stuff, taste what the world has to offer you.

'Dream-building' should be a part of your routine. Look around you at all the thousands of different lives people live. We get so used to our own that we often don't see how others live. All such different lives to us and the crazy thing is it's in our power, in our hands to change the life we currently have. One way is to do a completely different job.

As creatives we do have to remember that we need to keep moving forward, trying new things and experiences so we don't get bored. It may be that, at the moment, you can't see the bigger things in life and that's ok just get out there and keep 'dream-building' until you do. In the meantime, set yourself some goals that you can see and would like to aspire to. It could be a holiday, or a car or a promotion or a guitar or basically anything your heart desires.

Once you have something, however big or small, then we can reverse engineer achieving it. Firstly, we need to know what it costs and that might be in money terms or effort or both. If we want a holiday, then we need to cost it out so we can see how much extra money we will need to be able to afford it. We can then look at how we will earn that extra cash and plan the time and find the job to do the extra work that will fund it.

We simply break down everything to smaller and smaller increments until we have a plan of action that we can follow. One of the advantages of being a planet brain is we can normally see enough of the bigger picture to make that plan happen.

Top tip: Draw yourself a diagram that shows the steps towards your goals. Rather like the sort of thing people do when they are raising funds to repair the church roof, a visualisation of where you are at any point adds to the excitement as you see your goal getting nearer.

This is the same with all aspects of your life. Sitting staring at a computer screen playing games is not going to get you to meet people and build relationships. If you want to find 'the one' then get off your *can't* and put a plan in place to really go places. Make yourself join in with things and join organisations where the sort of person you'd like to meet is likely to be at.

What if I'm a strong introvert? You will find other introverts who have the same passions and interest that you do, you don't have to join in things that extraverts do.

"But Steve, I don't have the time!"

A bit of tough love. Stop being a 'settle for', settling for this, settling for that. You are a creative, a NUT. Settling for stuff is not an option for you. Choose your priorities. Build the life you want. The life you desire.

It's like the word compromise. I love Kirsty and Phil, as I do the various TV home programmes they present. However, I really hate it when they go on about how people have to *compromise*. No, they don't! Don't be a dream stealer! Yes, at this moment in time, we may not be able to get everything we want. That doesn't mean we give up on our perfect dreams.

A compromise is the acceptance of a standard lower than desirable.

As a creative it's our job to change stuff, to take the undesirable and make it wonderful. If, in our lives, we are living with stuff that is undesirable then don't just settle for it. Decide what you want, reverse engineer it, and put in a plan in place to change it, whatever it is. You have the power!

A question for you:

Three frogs sat on a wall; one decides to jump off. So how many are left?

The answer: Three. He *decided* to do it but, he didn't actually jump. Don't be a slave to procrastination. Planning is a waste of time if we do not take the action necessary to complete the task.

Another trait we NUTs can have is to spend so much time planning that we actually don't do anything.

Analyse to paralyse!

This is most often caused by fear. So, let's go on now to talk about how to Handle and Understand those fears.

STEVE FAVELL

CHAPTER 13

HANDLING AND UNDERSTANDING FEAR

Florence lived in a mid-terrace, two up two down, in a small town in Lancashire. Number 22, Argyle Street. She never locked her front door, why should she? After all, a neighbour might drop in for a chat or to borrow a cup of sugar. Flo, as she was known, knew everyone in the street. It had been only a year since her Ron had passed away and they had all been there for her. Even the coalman and milkman turned up for Ron's funeral.

Sitting by the open fire she liked to look out of the window and watch the children playing in the street. Flo was one of the first in Argyle Street to get a telephone. It was still exciting when the telephone rang as it was always a much-loved friend or relation, she could have a chat with. The local paper was delivered just before the postman came each day. Flo loved to keep up with the good things happening in the news and to read the letters from her family who didn't live close by. Life for Flo was simple, but she could go to bed each night satisfied she had done a good job and that all was well in her world.

Brian lives in a mid-terrace, two up two down, in a small town in Lancashire. Number 22 Argyle Street. With all the bad news about violence and break-ins he constantly sees on his 22" plasma TV, he followed his insurance company's advice and had locks fitted on all his windows and doors. He also has a deadlock and a chain on his front door.

Brian kind of knows the lady next door but that is about it. Like most of the other people who live in Argyle Street, he keeps himself to himself. Brian is a widower. His wife Jenny passed two years ago, leaving him to bring up their young children. Brian's children want to play in the street. With all the cars parked nose-to-tail, half on the pavement, coupled with Brian's fear of his children being harmed by a stranger, he daren't let them. Instead, they spend most of their time watching their TVs in their bedrooms. If he did let them roam outside, how would this look when social services checked on him?

No one from the street came to Jenny's funeral. Brian needs a phone for the internet for the children's homework. He also needs it just in case he has to call the doctors. However, when it rings, he never answers his phone, unless he is expecting someone. Why? Because of all the damn scam calls! Brian doesn't have milk delivered. When he did, it was often stolen, or the bottles left smashed on his doorstep. He doesn't take a paper, mainly because the last time he did it was full of negative news and sensational stories. Other than Christmas and birthdays, any post he gets goes straight onto the fire. Afterall it's all sales bumph! If someone knocks on Brian's door, he ignores them. It is nearly always someone trying to sell him something. Brian has high blood pressure, depression and goes to bed each night full of fears.

Florence lived in a mid-terrace, two up two down, in a small town in Lancashire, number 22, Argyle Street in the mid '60s. Brian lives in the same house today. Life has changed.

Yes, living standards and opportunities are much better today and yes, we are right to take precautions and be aware of any dangers. However, we are now subjected to so much information feeding our fears and social status, that fear and social anxiety has become an epidemic.

Our brains are very clever things indeed, but they are also programmable.

If a madman is actually standing in front of us waving a knife at us, we are right to be afraid and run away. However, most of the things we are afraid of do not exist, they are not real. We conjure up scenarios in our minds rather like plays. Plays of what might happen, what could happen, and these are most often dangers that evoke our fight or flight mode. Our fears, as we call them, are just scenarios we dream up. They are plays of scenarios we have created in our minds, and they are not real. They don't exist. We are painting pictures in our minds, dreaming up nightmare situations however unlikely, of what might happen. Chances are, they never will and even if they did, the outcome is unlikely to be anywhere near as bad as we are imagining it to be.

The biggest reason we procrastinate is that we come up with all sorts of negative scenarios in our minds. We go through, in our minds, how we will be judged or what could happen. In truth that probably never will happen and so we go into flight mode. Because of this we avoid doing the very things we *should* be doing.

"Steve there is a huge spider in the bath!" That's a call from my wife to remove it for her. When I get to the bathroom there sits a tiny little, frightened baby spider that literally couldn't hurt a fly. Silly thing is, I remove it for her which isn't actually helping her. Why? Because I am allowing her to avoid her fear. As such, I am reinforcing the scenario in her mind that it is going in some way to harm her.

Fear and anxiety are linked. So many people these days suffer with social anxiety. This comes in many forms, one of these is phone phobia, the fear of talking on the phone, I bet you know people who have this fear.

Social anxiety: **A fear of how people will judge us and what they will think of us.**

Just like the fear of spiders or anything else. We dream up unreal movies in our minds of what might happen, that, in reality never, ever will. The natural way we deal with this is to avoid doing the very things we have fears of. But in doing so, all we are doing is reinforcing our negative imaginings. We program our own brains by what we do and the experiences we have. Therefore, when we avoid that which we have a fear of, which is not real, all we are doing is programming our brains to believe it.

What we believe effects the action we put in. The result is therefore, what we expect, which in turn reinforces further our fear. Now if we change one thing and make ourselves deal with the spider, the result is it didn't eat us or poison us.

Now, however hard it was, we start to re-train our brain to believe that it is not a large threat. The more we take this action and face our fears, the easier it gets, until no longer does picking up a spider bother us.

If we chose to do so, we are more than capable of coming up with positive images. Scenarios of how wonderful an outcome could be. This is the key to dealing with fear. When we get negativity popping into our minds, we have to learn to stop the 'stinking thinking' we discussed previously and instead consciously dream up positive outcomes. Now we can make ourselves take action towards those positive outcomes.

Remember when you find yourself asking Why? Just add the word *not* = Why Not?

STEVE FAVELL

CHAPTER 14
MAKING YOUR PERFECT EXISTENCE

There is a huge difference between being rich and being wealthy. Working in the music industry I came across lots of people who were rich. They had more money than they knew what to do with and lived extravagant lifestyles. However, in my experience, many were desperately unhappy. Being wealthy is a state of mind. Yes being in control of your finances, being able to pay the bills does make a big difference but, being wealthy is being happy, content, feeling fulfilled and valued. Today, many of my friends are I believe, wealthy. They may not have very much money, but they feel they have a purpose in life. They look forward to getting up each day and doing what they do. They enjoy and value the relationships they have developed for themselves.

One thing I learnt travelling to different parts of the world is how so many people, who have very little, still have so much. So much happiness, joy, love and fulfilment in their lives. They have a sense of belonging and family. I think it is sad that so many of us have lost this sense of community. People are living their lives often not even getting to know their next-door neighbours.

For us NUTs this can be a particular challenge. On the one hand we've already discussed how we are often loaners, happy in our own company and thoughts. We are often seen, or see ourselves, as being different. Therefore, we can find it hard to fit in and feel valued. On the other hand, most of us need praise and encouragement and stimulating conversations with others.

Being wealthy is an area us NUTs have to work on. Fundamentally people are most interested in themselves. Even though you probably have a brain the size of a planet, a vast knowledge on most everything and a real talent for problem solving, chances are 90% of people will find you annoying unless you let them constantly talk about themselves most of the time.

I wonder if you have had this. You're in a group of people, and a loved one you are with might actually stop you talking or making a point at times saying, "You're boring them now." or "Will this explanation take long?" Yes, that's really rude and annoying to you and me but, we probably accept it, knowing we do have a tendency to go into more detail than the average person has the capacity to handle.

For balance in our relationships, us NUTs need to seek out other NUTs who we can have meaningful in-depth, grown-up conversations with. People who 'get you' and can talk about interesting stuff rather than just the latest soap on the TV. We do need to remember though, when seeking out other NUTs, that as NUTs themselves they may also have mood swings. Therefore, it could be challenging to have a relationship with them. Remember we want them to be understanding and sympathetic to us when we go off on one don't we? So, let's make an effort and allowances for their differences too.

Question: Who do you know that you could give yourself the gift of making friends with that will really stimulate you?

When it comes to making relationships with most others, I've had to learn to listen far more and dial down how much I say. In my younger days, I was getting a reputation for being 'full of it' or coming across as arrogant. I remember when I was at school a teacher once put on my report that I have 'verbal diarrhoea'. I think I still resemble that remark! Therefore, it's still a work in progress.

Being truly wealthy also requires another word and that is security. This of all things is the hardest. Security requires not only financial stability but also security in our relationships and health. The first, finance, we can make strides to have in our control. We can build a stable income and reserves and be prudent with our spending.

The second, relationships, we can and should constantly work on, never taking a relationship for granted and always seeking to make those relationships stronger. However, whilst we can do everything possible to keep ourselves fit, the third, health, can be a matter of pure luck.

For the most part I don't believe in luck as it's when preparation meets opportunity. You put yourself in the right place at the right time. You plan for what you want and look for opportunities as they come up. Then rather than procrastinate, you take action to use those opportunities. Yes, the harder you work the luckier you will get. You will make things happen even though others may just see what you achieve as good luck.

But where health is concerned, as long as we are not abusing our bodies or subjecting ourselves to unnecessary dangers, then chance does play a large part in how our lives will play out. That said, it's how we deal with our obstacles that defines who we are. There is no doubt that our mindset has a real influence over aspects of our health.

The actor Sir Michael Caine once did a TV interview with Michael Parkinson. During the interview he described how, in his early career, he had to walk through a door onto stage where two people were pretending to have a heated argument. The director had told the actors to adlib the argument, to make it spontaneous and therefore more realistic. During rehearsals, one of the actors threw a chair across the stage which lodged itself across that doorway so, when Michael came to enter, he found his entrance blocked. He said to the director, "Sorry I can't get in." Michael just stood there, not knowing what to do. Seeing Michael standing helpless in the doorway the director shouted at him, "USE THE DIFFICULTY!" The director went onto explain, "If it's a comedy or farce then fall over the chair, make it funny. If it's a drama then pick it up and smash it, but <u>always use the difficulty</u>!"

Sir Michael said he took this into every aspect of his life and now even his children say it. Whenever something bad happens, always say to yourself, 'Use the difficulty!' Think what can we get out of this? Sir Michael's philosophy is that nothing in this world is ever so bad that you cannot, in some small way, use that difficulty so that you're ahead, and you didn't let it get you down.

The perfect existence is to become mentally wealthy. By that I mean doing the best we can with the talents and health we have. To see difficulties as challenges and use them to build our self-worth by overcoming them.

STEVE FAVELL

CHAPTER 15
CREATING ANOTHER LIFETIME THAT STARTS TODAY

A dear friend kept saying this to me, "In another lifetime, perhaps?"

I had confided how I felt and what was wrong with my life at that time. At that time, I hadn't seen that I could change it. Each time I said I wanted to do this, or I moaned about my lot I simply got the same answer, "In another lifetime, perhaps?" But eventually the penny dropped, and I got it.

We can all look back to when we were very young and relied on our parents and others to look after us and we remember some things from those days. However, unless we try very hard, we probably don't really remember very much from then. Next, we have our teenage years and again in later life we look back. If you think about it, each phase of our lives is like 'another lifetime.' After a while, it's even hard for us to imagine that we were the person that lived that part of our past lives.

This can be especially true of past relationships we've had but we let them go and moved on. We know it was us, we can remember certain bits of it, but once we have let that 'lifetime' go it becomes hard to imagine ourselves in that position, in that relationship, in that phase of our lives. Often, we even wonder how we could have let ourselves be in that position in the first place.

When we go on holiday and have a wonderful time, after a while the memory of that holiday becomes a sort of nice dream. We smile when we look back at the photos remembering stuff we had long forgotten, don't we?

Dumping the negative and stating a new 'lifetime', a new chapter in our lives is something we can control. Something we can do if we choose to. We can see it for ourselves when we let go of one relationship and fall in love with someone else. It may not have happened over night but eventually we let go of the old and embraced the new, forgetting how it used to be. Now living in and experiencing our new existence, full of the *now* and the feelings and emotions that we now feel. Sometimes when we are in a bad place in our lives and we decide to change things, it can happen almost overnight.

If our lives are not at any moment what we would like them to be, we have the power to change it. We have that power to start a new lifetime living as we want to. Just as with other phases of our lives, that which we did not like about ourselves, or others will become a distant memory. However, when we move from one lifetime to another we can, if we chose to, take with us pain, fear, guilt and the negative way we value and see ourselves. If we do this, we simply compound whatever hang ups we have.

At times in our lives, we do stuff or have done stuff to us that deeply effects and shapes us in that 'lifetime'. The point is, it's a choice, yes some of this stuff remains with us but at any time we can choose to start building a new 'lifetime' leaving at least most of our challenges behind. By doing this eventually we will look back and find it hard to believe we had those challenges.

The issue in doing this is, however, the fear of the unknown.

On a business trip I visited a man in his home. He had an old dog sitting in the corner of the room. As we spoke, the dog suddenly let out a yelp and a moan, a sort of pained howl. As a dog lover myself, it sounded to me as though the dog was in dreadful pain. However, it was his dog and he ignored it, so I did as well and we carried on speaking. After a while the dog did cry out again. Again, he ignored it, so we carried on talking. When the dog cried out for a third time, I felt I had to say something.

I said, "I hope you don't mind me saying, but your dog sounds like he's in pain." The man replied, "Oh he is."

I was perplexed. So, I said, "Oh I'm so sorry? Whatever is wrong with him?"

The man said casually, "Stupid dog, he's sat on a nail." I naturally pulled an inquisitive face and said, "Surely that must hurt?"

The man replied, "Yes, but not enough to get off it yet!"

In life we can be in an uncomfortable position, even suffering pain of one sort or another but, we find ourselves in what is called a comfort zone. Sounds stupid, doesn't it? The fact is that a comfort zone can be very uncomfortable, full of pain and anguish, but it's what we know. It's what we are used to and, for us NUTs who are used to being different, we can imagine and dream up scenarios where, after all, we deserve this pain and discomfort – don't we?

Look how people live in abusive and violent relationships, where they are being regularly subjected to mental and physical abuse. You'd think they would leave and get out of the situation. How often do you hear that until that abuse gets beyond a certain point, most often, they don't?

Look at how people get hooked on drugs and drink, or smoking, or eating so much they become dangerously obese. Some people can get to a stage where they are hating themselves for who they have become, but seem unable to break the cycle.

If it's time for you to start a new 'lifetime,' take heart. There are millions of examples of people who have done just that. Reformed addicts who now live happy, fulfilled lives. Millions who had been in abusive violent relationships who now have a safe, loving, caring life. Millions who have given up smoking, drinking and are now proud of their body image. Millions of people who have found their purpose in life, who have gained self-worth and pride.

There are also millions of NUTs who have overcome their demons, their challenges. NUTs who have learnt to live with and make use of their differences in a positive way and have found peace. It all starts with just one step, then another, then another. The fear of the unknown is just another excuse we have for painting negative movies in our heads, creating a fear of what might happen.

The answer? When you're stuck in a hole they say, stop digging! Start to paint those positive movies in your head. Think instead about how wonderful your life could and will be. Stop and ask yourself for once… What do I want?

We can spend so much time concerned with what others think and how they will judge us, that we forget to simply ask ourselves this question…**What do I want?**

STEVE FAVELL

CHAPTER 16
HOW TO DEVELOP REAL WISDOM

As NUTs some of us fall into the trap of believing we are especially wise. We can think that our knowledge is often superior to others. In some ways it's true to say, many of us do have the capacity to have a greater than average, more in-depth knowledge on a subject. However, knowledge is not in any way, shape, or form the same as wisdom.

To fully understand what wisdom is, we first need to look at how, we as human beings, take in and process information.

Try this exercise. Keep looking forward at something, extend your arms out in front of you and wiggle your fingers. Even though you are focused on the thing in front of you, you can also see your wiggling fingers, yes? Now palms up, wiggling your fingers as you then slowly, still with arms outstretched, take your arms back as far as you can, to the side/behind yourself. Keep focused on the thing in front of you and see how far back you can take your arms and still see your wiggling fingers in your peripheral vision.

Amazing, isn't it? We can concentrate on one thing, but our eyes are still watching so much more and sending this information to the brain. This is the same with all of our other senses. How often have you sat in a restaurant or busy place, full of noise, having a discussion with someone, whilst also earwigging, picking out of the hubbub around you. At the same time, listening to someone else's juicy tale from their conversation? Our ears hear much more than we realise and send that data to our brain. We simply focus on what our brain chooses to listen to.

Have you considered how you can so often identify what you are eating simply by what it tastes like, or even how it smells? The receptors in our mouths and nose are incredible. They are sending constant data to the brain and let's not forget, all the data from the touch of our hands and the sensation on our skin. How we feel hot and cold, hard and soft and the difference even between the feel of the skin of one person to another.

In fact, as explained by Robert Harrison an internationally recognised trainer and developer in the areas of NLP, Coaching, Hypnosis, and Personality Profiling, *the average brain takes in two million bits of information per second from our senses.* Remember as NUTs the amount you take in, is likely to be higher because of the potential increase in the numbers of receptors *you* have going to *your* brain.

The challenge is, the brain can only handle and process about 134 thousand bits of information per second, that's only 6.7% of the two million bits per second it's receiving. Even if, as a NUT, your brain can handle more, it will never get close to the amount of information being sent to it. Instead, what we all do is this …

1.   We ignore and delete that which does not seem relevant to us.
2.   We distort and generalise the data.

It's like when we have a radio. The programmes and channels we are interested in, we tune into. If we like classical music, we tune into Classic FM and ignore Radio 1.

My wife and I decided to purchase a new car, well new to us at least. Together we searched the internet and found a nice, red, hybrid 4x4. Part of the appeal was that we hadn't seen many of them, especially in that colour. The very day we drove it away from the garage, suddenly it seemed like they were everywhere, even in the unusual red colour just like ours. The truth is, we just hadn't been tuned into them before.

Consider, how many times have you had an experience like that? It might be you got a dog and then when you took it to your local park, suddenly you noticed loads of other people had the same breed of dog as yours. Or it might have been an item of clothing you thought no one else had or even a building with a huge sign outside you pass every day on your commute to work. Until you had a bad back you didn't realise it was actually an osteopath.

In the same way we choose what data to take on board, we also distort and generalise data to fit our narrative. We even say things like, 'This tastes like that', 'That looks just like' or 'This feels or smells or seems like. We generalise with music, saying that's country or pop or rock or R&B. We generalise with art, we even stereotype the people we meet.

In our brains we each have a large memory bank. That memory bank is made up of past experiences, some real, some from what we have read or watched on TV or in films. Some of which comes from what we have learnt. Our personality type has a lot to do with what is in our memory banks too. If we, for instance, are far more of an introvert than an extrovert then we may see quiet time alone as more valuable. Whereas an extrovert might see that as loneliness. What we do is to compare the data we are receiving from our senses with the information in our memory banks. We put data into neat categories to make it easier to pick out what is of value to us. In doing so, as well as ignoring a lot of data, we also distort data to fit into a category. Basically, we lump data together and generalise.

A question for you: have you ever had an argument over something you and another person had seen or done, and you were both totally convinced you were right? Chances are, in that experience, you had each taken in the data to have a different meaning. For example: "He said this, I know what he meant, and it hurt my feelings!" "No, that's not what he was saying what he meant was this!" Same words or actions but totally different perspectives.

We compare the data we are receiving with the information in our memory banks. From this we make up our minds about what something means and the value it has to us.

The point here is, we are all different. How we interpret data from our senses is always different. We each have our own perspective on the world around us and we fundamentally see things differently.

The way we each see the meaning of that around us affects the way we feel. Remember, our feelings are our shortcuts which we use to make decisions. Our actions and responses are therefore a result of this process.

But what, you might say, has this to do with wisdom?

I was inspired by a story on YouTube by Spiritual Facilitator and Storyteller, Nithya Shanti. He explained ...

There were two young men, students of life, living and studying in a remote spiritual community. Home for them for three years was a beautiful monastery, perched on top of a high mountain, with a steep, rocky, winding path. To reach it took challenging days on foot, with an experienced guide to get there. Once there, in every direction the vista was stunning. Looking down, untouched by human hand, rolling hills stretched out as far as the eye could see with lush vegetation forming a canopy of deep green leaves, only broken by thin, glistening rivers, deep dark valleys and distant mountain tops.

Above, the vast sky remained for most of the year translucent, light blue, like an open door to the heavens with just occasional wisps of fluffy clouds drifting past then disappearing in the distance. At night the stars filled the void, twinkling and dancing in the moonlight. Food was plentiful, home was basic but comfortable and life was good.

The two young men were indeed fortunate and not just for their lifestyle. This monastery had, as its leader, a great and very wise master. He had many students but one day these two young men got into an argument. They both had different perspectives on an aspect of the teaching, and they started to argue. One said, "I'm right!" The other young man said, "No I'm right!" They simply couldn't agree, so the argument got more and more intense. Finally, one of them said, "I think we should go and ask the Master." The other replied, "Yes, I will go and ask the teacher."

So, the first young man went to the great hall where the master was sitting contemplating deep thoughts. He bowed down to the master and said, "Master, me and this other student were having this discussion, he said this, and I said that. My argument is logical and consistent and his is not, am I not right?"

The master looked up, smiled at him and said, "You're right."

Satisfied, the student went back to the other and laughing at him said, "See, the Master said I'm right, what were you thinking?"

The other student couldn't believe it, how could that be? He replied, "Let me go and ask him." So, he went to the master, bowed down and said, "Master, what he is saying is not based on fact, what I am saying is, surely I'm right?"

The master smiled back at him and said, "You're right."

So, the second student went back to the first student and he said, "See, the Master said I'm right!"

Perplexed the first student said, "How can that be? He said I'm right, now he says that you are right; it doesn't make sense." So, they both went to the master and bowed down. The first student began, "Master, you told me I'm right but then he told you something completely different and you said he's right. We can't both be right!"

The master's face beamed at them both and he said, "You're right."

The message of this story is, when we get fixated on "I'm right, I'm right!" it always leads to a fight!!

We only see things from our point of view. A point of view is always limited. It is never comprehensive. The way I visualise the monastery in the story is bound to be different to the way you visualise it reading this book. The way you see the room you are in is bound to be different from the way others see it. We each compare the information we are taking in through our senses and compare it to personal experiences we have had in the past to give us meaning.

A simple picture on a wall, will for many, evoke a memory from the past and they will associate that room with that event. Each person who has that reaction will have a completely different association and reaction. Some will be positive, happy thoughts, for others it might conjure up hurt. For many others, the picture will simply be a picture and will be ignored, not even noticed or remembered.

I recently went to a vintage coffee shop. The whole place was styled to look like a 1940's war tearoom. Even the staff were dressed in period costume. For me it evoked memories of my parents and grandparents. There was a picture on the wall of King George, the same picture which had been on my grandmother's wall which I remember as a child visiting her home. The plates, knives, forks and spoons to me all seemed familiar. Tea was poured from a tea pot with a knitted, woollen jacket, through a tea strainer, just like I remember as a child growing in the '60s. It felt warm and comforting, bringing back happy associations.

However, for the elderly lady in the corner who had been taken there by her grandchildren as a treat; it bought floods of tears and sadness. Something in that room, perhaps the whole room evoked memories of losing both her parents and her brother during the blitz. Leaving her distraught. Her well-meaning family learnt not to ever make that association again.

How we each see something is just our individual knowledge, our perspective. Knowledge is just a point of view. Wisdom on the other hand is a viewing point. Wisdom is the ability to see things from many different perspectives not just our own.

Think about the story. The steep, rocky, winding path that took challenging days on foot with an experienced guide to get there was, for the students, an exhilarating journey of adventure. How would that have been for you if in real life you had to do it? A wonderful experience or your worst nightmare? In reality, if you were faced with it, how would you see living for three years in a monastery, perched on top of a high mountain? Living without any creature comforts, no electricity, mobile phone or TV? Would the view be beautiful or, a constant reminder of the total isolation of living in such a place?

Often when we read a story or watch a film, we can immerse ourselves in someone else's world. Often even seeing things and experiencing things from their point of view. However, if we were actually in that situation ourselves, we would most likely have a totally different perspective of what was happening around us. To us, our experience would be totally different.

80% of challenges are actually caused by a lack of communication.

Ask yourself, how often have you felt like you're not being listened to?

Have you had experiences when you are having an actual conversation with someone, and you get frustrated because you are totally aware they are not actually listening to what you are saying? It's like their head is stuck in their own point of view!

The master in the story was operating from wisdom, he was able to see things from one person's perspective and the other person's perspective which is why for him they were both truly right. To be wise is to operate from a position where we let go of our strong identification, our likes and dislikes and let go of our point of view.

Instead, learn to accept the different perspectives and points of view that others have. Learn to embrace how they see and experience things. Work collaboratively to understand how their perspective can work with your own. Then and only then can we have true connection, and a true understanding.

I have a genius friend called Jenny. Jenny was labelled at a very young age as having Asperger's Syndrome because she has difficulty with social interaction and tended to engage in repetitive behaviour.

She loves wild swimming and is really good at it which has always been a blessing for her parents Along with her other differences such as, having difficulty reading facial expressions, body language and social cues, she also has challenges with her motor skills like running and walking.

Jenny never lies, I don't think she can. Jenny stands firm on her opinions and beliefs and focuses a lot on rules and routines, the idea of breaking a rule is something she cannot and will not comprehend. Jenny has a brilliant mind, she is a first-class lawyer, ask her a question about rules, about the law, about facts and figures and she can quote word for word relevant passages from every book she has ever read on the subject and believe me she reads a lot!

One summer out with her parents as a young girl, Jenny went wild swimming, she was having so much fun but suddenly she stopped swimming and started to get into real difficulty. Panic struck, her father plunged himself into the cold water and dragged his precious daughter back to the safety of the riverbank. Once on dry land and with Jenny wrapped up warm away from danger, her parents asked, "What happened Jenny? You are such a good swimmer how come you nearly drowned?!" "I wasn't allowed" Jenny simply said.

She explained, "I swam underwater then when I came up as looked at you, I could see a sign in the bullrushes which read, 'No Swimming'.

Words are such powerful things and just like all the other information we process, we each have our own perspective on their value and meaning.

Having previously said that we each fundamentally see things differently, we also need to consider how this principle also applies to the meaning we have of what we read and the way we interpret what is said when someone speaks to us.

You might think that this is a challenge that you don't have but, don't deceive yourself; this is an issue everyone has.

Take this sentence:

"I didn't say he stole your money."

Ask yourself, what is the message in the sentence, what is the writer saying?

"I didn't say he stole your money."

Now let's look at the effect of emphasising each word. Firstly, emphasise the first word and read the sentence again:

"**I** didn't say he stole your money."

For most people, simply by emphasising the first word "**I**", the meaning of the sentence becomes that I didn't say it but that someone else may have said it.

Now let's do the same with the word **Didn't:**

"I **Didn't** say he stole your money."

This time the sentence becomes a denial, as though someone had accused me of saying it, but it wasn't me.

How about if we emphasise the word **Say:**

"I didn't **say** he stole your money."

Now it's indicating that I may have inferred it, but I didn't actually say it.

When emphasising the word, **He:**

"I didn't say **he** stole your money."

The sentence is now saying that it wasn't him that I said stole it, it was someone else.

"I didn't say he **stole** your money." becomes that yes, I accused him of taking it but, not necessarily, stealing it.

"I didn't say he stole **your** money." would most likely be taken as I was accusing him of stealing someone else's money.

"I didn't say he stole your **money.**" becomes that he stole something else from you other than money.

The way we interpret what we read is totally dependent on the way we read it and the bias we put on it at the time. This is also true of the meaning we take from what is said to us and often as humans we get this wrong.

We misunderstand the message someone is trying to convey and instead read into a sentence some unintended implication. It's why we should never judge a person or a situation on text alone and it's something we should consider when, for instance we are writing a CV or doing a job application.

Often someone who does not know us, will read into a paragraph we have written, something unintended. The art here is to get others, preferable others who do not know you very well, to critique your application and wherever possible we should talk to people face to face so that, not only can they hear your words to gain meaning, but can also see your body language and give you the opportunity to explain.

You may have heard of the 7-38-55 rule? This is a concept concerning the communication between people. The rule states that on average, only 7% of meaning is actually communicated through what is said. Much more important is the way we say it, with 38% of communication being through your tone of voice and the inflections you use. With face-to-face communication, a massive 55% of communication is actually through body language and for some of us NUTs this can be a real challenge.

Many of us do not display what is considered typical body language. In face-to-face situations, many NUTs feel awkward or nervous whilst others can come across as overconfident, possibly even aggressive or arrogant.

The secret here is to remember people make decisions on the way we make them feel. Even if we do not have typical body language, we can still get others to like and engage with us. If we always make a point of being interested in them, praising them, asking them questions, actively listening and making them feel valued.

Rather than us talking all the time and showing how brilliant we are.

We cannot change other people, but we can actively listen to them. Really listen and look to understand how they see things and experience things. Then we can change what we do to influence their actions. That is wisdom.

STEVE FAVELL

AFTERWORD

I hope that in some small way my ramblings have been of some value in your life's journey. I'd like to leave you with this final thought ...

As creatives we tend to do something especially nutty!!

We give ourselves tasks to do all the time to stop ourselves being creative. To stop ourselves doing the things we want!

Often this goes into the realms of compulsive behaviour, like cleaning all the time when we don't really need to. We take work with us on holiday and fill our days with stuff *we have to do*. We even feel guilty taking time out to relax and be creative.

A lot of this is about control. We do stuff because that way we feel we are in control of, at least part of, our lives. Instead take control in a constructive way.

In Douglas Adams book *"The Hitchhiker's Guide to the Galaxy"* he had a robot called Marvin.

Marvin was the spaceship's robot - one of the ones Douglas called the Sirius Cybernetics Corporation's *GPP* (Genuine People Personalities) robots. Poor Marvin suffered with depression and also boredom.

He had a "brain the size of a planet" but the challenge was he was never able to use it. Instead, the crew got him doing mundane tasks like opening doors.

A typical comment from Marvin was, "Here I am with a brain the size of a planet and they ask me to pick up a piece of paper! Call that job satisfaction? I don't!"

As a NUT, you may also have a brain the size of a planet and just like Marvin, if you don't use it then you will get bored, have a lack of job satisfaction and probably get depressed.

The thing is, you're the one with the brain the size of a planet so *you* are the only one who can understand all the wonderful things you can do and achieve. If you are just doing mundane tasks and jobs set by others, then, *you* are limiting yourself.

As creatives it is up to us to challenge ourselves, to stretch beyond the norm and keep ourselves engaged and enriched by using the immense power of our brains. So, take action and be creative!

I hope in your diary you put at least one day aside for you ...

- The 'one thing' that day.
- Time to be *you*.
- Time to be creative.
- Time to build your next 'lifetime'.

If you haven't, take control and do it now!

Today we live the dreams of yesterday.

Tomorrow, we live the life we build today.

Get a dream that's bigger than your obstacles because

Your next lifetime is just a decision step away

Steve Favell

ABOUT THE AUTHOR

Steve Favell is an experienced Business Training Consultant with an extensive history of helping businesses to grow and prosper. During his later career Steve specialised in the Education and Apprenticeships sector. He therefore enjoyed working with a wide range of clients including FE Colleges, and Private Providers.

Steve is also skilled in project management and the recruitment, management and training of national sales teams. As a much sought-after trainer with a portfolio of bespoke courses written for many topics, the most popular being Negotiation, Business Planning, Sales, Bid Writing, and Training Delivery, he also makes a fascinating after dinner speaker.

Follow him on LinkedIn /steve-favell

Printed in Great Britain
by Amazon